Power of Popular Piety

Power of Popular Piety

A Critical Examination

Ambrose Mong

Foreword by
Michael Amaladoss
and Patricia Madigan

CASCADE *Books* • Eugene, Oregon

POWER OF POPULAR PIETY
A Critical Examination

Copyright © 2019 Ambrose Mong. All rights reserved. Except for brief quotations in critical publications or reviews, no part of this book may be reproduced in any manner without prior written permission from the publisher. Write: Permissions, Wipf and Stock Publishers, 199 W. 8th Ave., Suite 3, Eugene, OR 97401.

Cascade Books
An Imprint of Wipf and Stock Publishers
199 W. 8th Ave., Suite 3
Eugene, OR 97401

www.wipfandstock.com

PAPERBACK ISBN: 978-1-5326-5643-9
HARDCOVER ISBN: 978-1-5326-5644-6
EBOOK ISBN: 978-1-5326-5645-3

Cataloguing-in-Publication data:

Names: Mong, Ambrose. |

Title: Power of popular piety : a critical examination / Ambrose Mong.

Description: Eugene, OR: Cascade Books, 2019 | Includes bibliographical references and index.

Identifiers: ISBN 978-1-5326-5643-9 (paperback) | ISBN 978-1-5326-5644-6 (hardcover) | ISBN 978-1-5326-5645-3 (ebook)

Subjects: LCSH: Folk religion. | Religion Christianity Catholic. | Religion and culture. | Social sciences.

Classification: GN470. M6 2019 (paperback) | GN470 2019 (ebook)

Manufactured in the U.S.A.   02/08/19

For Abraham Shek Lai-him, GBS, SBS, JP

They who are not superstitious without the Gospel, will not be religious with it.
—John Henry Newman

Contents

Foreword by Michael Amaladoss and Patricia Madigan | ix
Preface and Acknowledgements | xv
Introduction | xvii

Chapter 1
Popular Piety | 1

Chapter 2
Our Lady of Guadalupe | 20

Chapter 3
Pinoy Piety | 41

Chapter 4
Accommodation and Inculturation | 61

Chapter 5
Superstition and Piety | 79

Chapter 6
Our Lady of Medjugorje | 97

Chapter 7
Sacred Heart and Divine Mercy | 116

Epilogue | 141

Bibliography | 147
Index | 157

Foreword

by Michael Amaladoss, SJ
and Patricia Madigan, OP

Michael Amaladoss, SJ

All of us know what popular piety is because almost all of us practice it at sometime or another. We go on pilgrimages to sacred shrines. We join celebrations of local festivals. We participate in family or group rituals associated with cosmic or life cycles. But we may not always have been fully aware of its significance in our lives. It is so much a part of our lives that we take it for granted. Even those who do not go regularly to church rituals may find popular piety attractive. Ambrose Mong, through this rather small volume, *Power of Popular Piety: A Critical Examination*, is offering us an occasion to reflect upon it.

Popular piety may be looked at from different points of view. The term *popular* may be contrasted with the "elite." The spiritual "elite" are busy with the practice of silent meditation or contemplation. The people, on the contrary, engage in pilgrimages, novenas, and noisy celebrations. "Popular" may also be differentiated from the "official." The priests are occupied with their liturgical books and carefully orchestrated rituals. The people are more spontaneous. They improvise their prayers and use all sorts of symbolic gestures and objects. They are the agents of their celebrations. They do not need priestly mediators. They need not go to an official place of worship. They can do it at home or in the field or in the work place.

Aloysius Pieris suggests a distinction between cosmic and metacosmic religions and rituals. Cosmic religions deal with life in the world and deal with the forces of nature, which may sometimes be personified as spirits. Metacosmic religions reach out to the transcendent in various forms. From this point of view, popular piety may be classified as cosmic. But this may not be an adequate identification. Even cosmic rituals may imply, at some moments, a metacosmic dimension, though it may not be too explicit. Metacosmic religions may often operate at cosmic levels. Popular piety, for instance, does involve supernatural manifestations, apparitions, and miracles. In the Catholic tradition, for instance, we note, on the one hand, the apparitions of Jesus with his sacred and merciful heart and of Mother Mary. On the other hand, these are not manifestations of the transcendent divine but of its human forms of Jesus and Mary with their bodies and hearts, to which people can relate in a human way.

Another way of understanding popular piety is that its rituals and celebrations cater to various social occasions and needs that the official rituals do not attend to. The Catholic Church has seven sacramental celebrations. Five of them relate to key moments of life like birth, initiation to adulthood, marriage, etc. Only two concern ordinary ongoing life, namely the Eucharist and Reconciliation. These do not concern the life cycle, the cosmic cycle, the agricultural cycle, etc. There is a small book of blessings which is not very much used. Besides, people may feel that a priest may not be required to care for such personal and social needs. There are other rituals agents and community leaders available for these purposes. The people also feel free to evolve their own cultural symbols and rituals for the purpose. The official rituals are tied to a Latin cultural tradition which is not theirs. Efforts at inculturation—at least in Asia—initiated by missionaries like Matteo Ricci and Roberto de Nobili and others have not been encouraged. Popular rituals and celebrations fill this gap. The symbols and symbolic actions used in them are drawn from the cultures of the people in which they feel at home. So what we have in popular piety may be alternative and parallel rituals. People go to the priest and the church for an official initiation, marriage, or funeral ceremony. But the event is celebrated more elaborately at home or in the community. This happens all over the world, particularly in Africa, Asia, and Latin America, among people who still seek to live in harmony with the wider social group and the cosmos. Their worldview is not limited to that of the official Latin culture. Such celebrations are not absent even in Europe in rural areas. People tend to assert their agency and freedom. The official agents—priests—are not unaware of these. Sometimes they encourage popular piety because it brings more people to the church.

We often hear complaints that in some parts of the world people are moving away from the church to various Pentecostal movements. The reason is that they seem to be catering to personal, social, and emotional needs of people in a religious context, to which the traditional churches and their agents are not catering. This is often true also of popular piety.

Ambrose Mong starts his book with the theme of liberation. He seeks to show that Latin American liberation theologians, though they were critical of popular piety at an earlier stage, sought to give it a revolutionary perspective later. I do not know how successful they were. They were not emerging from the popular movements themselves. Perhaps they imposed their ideology on them. The recent history of Latin America seems to show that the liberation stream has lost its steam both at official and at popular levels.

But what is surprising in the many apparitions which are at the root of some forms of popular piety which Mong evokes in the book—the Sacred Heart, the Heart of Divine Mercy, Our Lady of Guadalupe, Our Lady of Medjugorje—is that they represent divine initiative. It is our Lord or our Lady who appear either to children or to an unlettered peasant or to simple religious locked up in their convents to give the world through them a message at a time and a place where and when such a message is urgently required. The "official" church may seek to downgrade it as a private revelation and approve it reluctantly (in the case of Medjugorje, for example). But the divine persons seem to take over, their involvement manifested by miracles, and they have a clear message to the church and to the world. This is obviously a sign that God continues to be present in our world and is concerned about us. From their fruits, we will know them. The church does not have a monopoly of facilitating divine-human encounter. This is true also of other apparitions like Lourdes and Fatima and others less known in other countries, like Velankanni in India. We can also think of the Black Madonnas in many countries in Europe and other popular saints all over the world. Popular piety acquires in this way a divine—metacosmic—dimension.

This realization also helps us to distinguish between two types of popular piety. One type refers to the rituals and celebrations that people create to cater to their personal and social needs. The other concerns pilgrimages and celebrations that emerge out of divine or saintly self-manifestations to which people respond. These challenge people to change personally and socially—the conversion that Mother Mary constantly talks about in her various apparitions. These are the forms of popular piety that Ambrose is presenting to us in this book.

I am very happy to congratulate Ambrose Mong on his book and welcome its publication. It is characterized by simplicity, clarity and depth. I hope that it will have a wide readership and provoke much reflection.

Michael Amaladoss, SJ, Institute of Dialogue with Cultures and Religions, Loyola College, Nungambakkam, Chennai, India.

***

Patricia Madigan, OP

In a conversation I once had with a Protestant pastor, she shared with me her observation that, in this age of declining formal Christian church membership in Australia, the Catholic Church, unlike her own church community, had the advantage of being characterized by numerous "levels" of conversation. When communication faded on one level—be it at the level of church leadership, doctrine, or perhaps liturgical practice—the faithful simply moved to another level of devotional engagement so that their basic Christian commitment remained stable despite the disruption.

But Catholics themselves have not always appreciated the depth of richness and engagement that popular piety or religiosity brings to their Christian tradition. Popular piety is often judged to be a hodgepodge of superstition, idolatry, or magic, a distorted understanding of the Christian mystery, a sop for the poor and ignorant. It can be easily dismissed as not culturally progressive. Some pastoral responses have discouraged or condemned it as drawing its adherents away from more conventional forms of religious belief and practice.

The post-Vatican II Catholic Church has manifested a certain ambivalence in its relationship with popular piety. It is recognized that popular religion has both the potential to become a resource for the fight for liberation against unjust social and economic structures, but also the possibility to be manipulated by those with an interest in protecting their power and privileges. The official Church has often been more supportive of the latter. Pope John Paul II was notoriously negative about the influence of a liberative theology in Latin America, where he believed it was distorting

Foreword

Christianity, although he supported it in the context of the political struggle in his homeland of Poland. However, often missing in these various pastoral responses is an attempt to understand the complex and multilayered meanings of popular Catholicism from the perspective of the practitioners.

As we experience a post-colonial globalized instability in the Christian project, we note also the rise of popular religion as a way in which ordinary people make sense of and identify with a religious tradition that, at an official level of doctrine or practice, no longer speaks to them. There is a growing recognition in the Catholic Church that popular expressions of faith centred on a religious symbol such as a particular apparition of the Madonna have the potential not only to reinforce identity and a sense of belonging, but also to give meaning to one's pain and suffering, and to become a force for change and the basis of liberation.

The phenomenon of popular piety is explored in this book by Ambrose Mong in several of its many inculturated forms, including in Mexico, Medjugorje, the Philippines, and China. As an assistant parish priest and part-time lecturer and researcher at the Chinese University of Hong Kong, who has spent time living in, India, Canada, Rome, and the Philippines as well as in China, he is well qualified to examine these many examples within the broad realm of Catholic tradition. He holds that popular piety, when properly understood and guided, can be a powerful force broadening and deepening political consciousness, and mobilizing people to act and bring gospel values to bear on their current situation.

In this he is very much within the framework of Catholic Church teaching as expressed by Pope Paul VI, who acknowledged the significance of the existence of these "particular expressions of the search for God and for faith" (*Evangelii Nuntiandi*, 48). Pope Francis has stated:

> Underlying popular piety, as a fruit of the inculturated Gospel, is an active evangelizing power which we must not underestimate: to do so would be to fail to recognize the work of the Holy Spirit . . . Expressions of popular piety have much to teach us; for those who are capable of reading them they are a *locus theologicus* which demands our attention . . . (*Evangelii Gaudium*, 126)

This book offers its readers such an opportunity to develop further a critical understanding and appreciation of the power of popular piety.

Dr. Patricia Madigan, OP, Executive Director of the Dominican Centre for Interfaith Ministry, Education and Research, Sydney, Australia.

Preface and Acknowledgements

There are a number of reasons why pilgrimages are popular in Hong Kong. Living in a crowded city and usually in small apartments, many Catholics feel the need to travel with their families and friends in the company of spiritual directors to places where they can pray and deepen their knowledge of the faith. The small but affluent Catholic community in Hong Kong allows them to travel with ease and comfort. A world-class airport and well-established tour companies are added advantages for pilgrims.

In fact, pilgrimages have become so popular and widespread that a number of priests involve themselves in leading the various groups as spiritual directors; they have to leave their parishes, each time lasting one to two weeks, three or four times a year. Unfortunately, this has affected the running of parishes where there is already a shortage of priests. Thus, on March 26, 2018, the Chancery Office has issued a notice regarding priests going on pilgrimages. The notice has decreed that with effect from April 1, 2018, priests working in parishes may join or lead pilgrimages outside Hong Kong no more than twice a year. While acknowledging that leading a pilgrimage is a form of pastoral ministry, the Chancery Office rightly insists that priests must give first priority to the parish ministry or other ministries they have been assigned to.

Be that as it may, this phenomenon reveals the emergence of popular piety in Hong Kong and many parts of Asia. Besides going on pilgrimages, novenas, devotions to the Blessed Virgin Mary, Divine Mercy, and processions on Feast days are also attended by the faithful with great enthusiasm.

Many people have assisted me in the writing of this book. First I wish to thank Professor Lai Pan-chiu and Henrietta Cheung for providing some of the books not easily available in Hong Kong libraries. Special thanks to Francis Chin, Columba Clearly OP, Scott Steinkerchner OP, Patrick Tierny FSC, Patrick Colgan SSC, Venny Lai, Hilia Chan, Kim Tansley, Kenzie Lau, and Adelaide Wong for proofreading and editorial assistance. I would also like to thank the following who have encouraged and supported me in my writing endeavors all these years: George Yeo, Peter Phan, Josephine Chan, Teresa Au, Vivencio Atutubo, Emmanuel Dispo, Rosalind Wong, Denis Chang SC, Philip Lee, George Tan, Michael Nerva, Patrick Chia, Anthony Tan, James Boey, Joseph Yim, Mary Cheung, Dominic Yeo-Koh FSG, Esther Chu, Tommy Lam, Emily Law, William Chan, Vivian Lee, Lea Lai, John K. S. Goh, Garrison Qian, Teoh Chin Chin, Wendy Wu, and Leo Tan.

Working in St. Andrew's Church, a very vibrant parish in Hong Kong, has given me many opportunities to reflect on the prevalence and power of popular piety. Thanks to the parish priest, Rev. Jacob Kwok, and my fellow colleagues, Fabio Favatta, PIME, and Mechelle Reginio, CICM, for sharing their experiences and insights on a host of issues regarding pastoral work and popular piety.

Last but not least, I owe my thanks to the superb staff at Cascade Books, especially Matthew Wimer, Rodney Clapp, Jesselyn Clapp, Ian Creeger, and Daniel Lanning. Special thanks to Robin Parry for his encouragement and support.Any shortcomings in this volume are my own.

Introduction

The inception of this volume, *Power of Popular Religion*, is derived from the *Directory on Popular Piety and the Liturgy* and the theology of liberation, which also has its origin in Latin America. Most writings on popular religiosity (*religiosidad popular*) such as devotions to Christ, the Blessed Virgin Mary, the saints, patronal feasts, and novenas are set within the context of Latin America. While many literary works on popular piety in the context of Latin America have been published, in this volume I have included the practice of popular religion in Asia and Eastern Europe.

In this work, the term *popular piety* is used synonymously with popular religiosity, popular religion, folk religion, common religion, or popular Catholicism. Popular piety by no means suggests that Christianity is trendy or fashionable; instead, it is defined as devotional rituals that originated from and are practiced by the common people, as opposed to church-sanctioned liturgical worship. In actuality, the church encourages popular pieties provided they conform to Canon laws and local regulations. The *Constitution of the Sacred Liturgy* states: "these devotions should be so drawn up that they harmonize with the liturgical seasons, accord with the sacred liturgy, are in some fashion derived from it, and lead the people to it, since, in fact, the liturgy by its very nature far surpasses any of them."[1]

In the years following Vatican II (1962–1965), we witnessed a decline in the practice of popular piety such as devotions to the Sacred Heart of Jesus and the Immaculate Heart of Mary, processions celebrating patronal feasts and novenas. However, there was a revival of popular religion in both developing countries as well as developed ones in the late twentieth century. In addition to trips to Jerusalem and Rome, pilgrimages to Marian Shrines, such as Fatima, Lourdes, and Medjugorje are extremely popular among

---

1. *Sacrosanctum Concilium*, no. 13.

Introduction

Hong Kong Catholics. These are mostly Catholics who have retired with the means and luxury of time to deepen their faith through such journeys.

Why was there a resurgence of popular piety? One leading explanation is that the faithful find the church liturgy rather dull and monotonous. Church worship has not been able to successfully respond to the emotional and psychological needs of the congregation. Perhaps this is the reason many Christians have flocked to Pentecostalism or charismatic renewal, which emphasizes the power of the Holy Spirit as being spontaneous and joyful. People want to feel and experience God working in their lives. In the nineteenth century, a German theologian, Friedrich Schleiermacher (1768–1834), equated religion with intuition, a motivating force, and a feeling of absolute dependence. He writes: "Your feeling is piety in so far as it is the result of the operation of God in you by means of the operation of the world upon you . . . These feelings are exclusively the elements of religion."[2] Thus, "the sum total of religion is to feel that, in its highest unity, all that moves us in feeling is one; to feel that aught single and particular is only possible by means of unity; to feel . . . that our being and living is a being and living and in through God."[3] In other words, all sensations are pious except when the person is sick. For Schleiermacher, religion is founded neither on doctrine nor morality.

Views of two Pontiffs

Recognizing the sign of the times, two pontiffs have also encouraged the practice of popular piety provided that they are exercised in communion with the church. Pope Benedict XVI maintained that popular piety, rooted in faith, serves as an excellent tool for the new evangelization in Latin America. When channeled properly, these practices can lead to a fruitful encounter with God, a deep reverence for the Eucharist, profound devotion to the Blessed Virgin Mary, and a cultivated love for the Church and its vicar. In other words, it helps to communicate faith, strengthen the bonds of friendship and family, and promotes solidarity and the exercise of charity. At the same time, Pope Benedict XVI also warned that popular piety cannot be merely a cultural expression of a specific religion, but must be grounded in faith and related to the Liturgy, that the encounter with the divine word must lead to a profound change of life and a radical identification

2. Schleiermacher, *On Religion*, 45–46.
3. Ibid., 49–50.

Introduction

with the message of Christ. He said "liturgy remains the primary reference point so as 'clearly and prudently to channel the yearnings of prayer and the charismatic life' which are found in popular piety."[4] Further, he added, "popular piety, because of its symbolic and expressive qualities, can often provide the Liturgy with important insights for inculturation and stimulate an effective dynamic creativity" . . . that "certainly popular piety always needs to be purified and refocused, yet it is worthy of our love and it truly makes us into the 'People of God.'"[5]

Pope Francis views popular piety as a means of transmitting the faith and cultivating it, and insists such pious practices must be exercised in communion with the hierarchy in order to maintain unity in the church. He told the crowd during mass at St. Peter Square on May 5, 2013, "Popular piety is a road which leads to what is essential, if it is lived in the Church in profound communion with your pastors . . . This is wonderful! A legitimate way of living the faith, a way of feeling that we are part of the Church." Popular piety thus lays out a path that leads to what is fundamental in our faith if lived in communion with the pastors of the church. Witnessing a variety of popular devotion, Francis said: "A great wealth and variety of expressions in which everything leads back to unity; the variety leads back to unity, and the unity is the encounter with Christ." The Pontiff addressed to the confraternities: "You have a specific and important mission, that of keeping alive the relationship between the faith and the cultures of the peoples to whom you belong. You do this through popular piety."[6] Pope Francis also highlights the importance of faith that comes from hearing the word of God, which also engages the senses, emotions, and symbols of different cultures.

Manifestations in Latin America and Asia

Latin American scholars have contributed significantly to the study of popular religion as a force for the transformation of society; they have achieved this while also underscoring the weaknesses and ambiguities that exist. Liberation theologians in Latin America initially believed that popular religion would eventually give way to a more evangelical or gospel-centered Christianity. In other words, the "conscientizing forces of liberation" would

4. Pope Benedict XVI, "Popular piety and the new evangelization," 4.
5. Ibid.
6. Pope Francis, *Holy Mass on the Occasion of the Day of Confraternities*.

Introduction

eventually replace pious practices of the people.[7] However, that was not the case. Popular piety is here to stay. In fact, in recent decades, we have experienced a resurgence manifesting in various forms.

As a prevalent form of Christian experience, popular piety cannot be easily erased from the lives of the people. In actuality, popular religion has enabled people to experience the divine since ancient times. Without doubt, there exists abuse in the practice of popular religion, such as superstitious beliefs and idolatry. Popular piety also promoted a fatalistic view of life that prevents the poor and the oppressed from surpassing the harsh realities they face. Such an approach was also adopted by other ideologies and religious traditions.

Marxists approach popular religion as a kind of false consciousness imposed by the ruling class on the working class. The dominant power either encourages the poor in religious devotion that promises reward in the afterlife, or forbids them from taking part in religious activities, which could heighten their social awareness of the societal injustice. The ruling class aims to maintain their status quo and keep the poor in their place. Regrettably, aside from a few prophetic voices, the church predominantly supports the status quo of such an establishment. Marxists thus call for a conscientization of the poor, empowering them with knowledge on the relationship between power and labor in society.

Extreme Marxists seek the destruction of religious beliefs. Liberation theologians, influenced by Marxism, are determined to "evangelize" popular religion by going back to the Scripture, focusing on the Word of God, which has the power to transform the individuals to actively fight against injustice. According to Francisco Vanderhoff, "One cannot 'evangelize' popular religion without demythologizing it, and one cannot demythologize it without politicizing its own environmentally conditioned sociopolitical relationships."[8] Liberation theologians are thus drawn into political frays, which sometimes create conflicts with the Vatican.

Popular piety also exists in other great religious traditions. In Mahayana Buddhism, devotion to Guan Yin (觀音), known as the "Goddess of Mercy," is immensely popular among East Asians. The name, *Guan Yin*, means "observing the sounds of the world" (聲音), revealing her ability to listen to the voices of the masses. One of the many images of Guan Yin displays her as a person with many arms, hands, and eyes, portraying her

---

7. Schreiter, *Constructing Local Theologies*, 122.
8. Ibid., 133.

Introduction

capability to protect the weak and the needy. In China, Guan Yin is often shown wearing a white flowing robe, necklaces, and carrying a jar of pure water in her right hand, and a willow branch in her left hand. Devotion to Guan Yin was brought to China from India during the first century AD, and this popular piety was farther spread to Japan and Korea.

In the early stage, Guan Yin appeared as a male Indian *bodhisattva Avalokiteśvara*. Over time, this male deity was transformed into a goddess because the female representation evokes the tender, compassionate, and merciful *Avalokiteśvara* more effectively. These traits of compassion and kindness are associated with the Chinese concept of *Yin* (陰), the feminine aspect of creation. By the twelfth century, as a result of Taoist influence on Buddhism, Guan Yin was portrayed in exclusively female form. Guan Yin's birthday is celebrated on the nineteenth day of the second lunar month.[9]

Outline and Sequence of the Work

Popular piety is neither intrinsically good or bad, but it is very powerful. Particular devotions as they are practiced in particular cultures can have net good and bad effects. Popular religion can have a greater influence on people's real, lived faith than any theological idea. Chapter 1 discusses the positive and negative aspects of popular piety. It also examines the relationship between liberation theology and popular religion, referencing examples in Latin America where both liberation theologians as well as the dominant class have used the practice of popular piety to advance their own agendas.

Chapter 2 examines the apparition of the Virgin of Guadalupe in its historical context, and the various interpretations and controversies surrounding this event. *Somos Mexicanos, Somos Gaudalupanos.* Namely, to be a devotee of Our Lady of Guadalupe is part of Mexican identity and national consciousness. This chapter also demonstrates that the conquest of Mexico was just as brutal and violent as the Aztec regime, which the Spanish conquistadors sought to destroy. Devotion to Our Lady of Guadalupe symbolizes a spiritual triumph for the native Mexicans when they appropriate the Iberian faith as their very own. In fact, Guadalupe becomes a sign of unity among various disparate groups in Mexican society.

As the only predominantly Roman Catholic nation in Southeast Asia, the Philippines can claim to be the center of popular folk Catholicism in

9. Guan Yin, *New World Encyclopaedia*.

this continent, and has preserved its popular Catholic devotions in modified form from days as a Spanish colony. In other words, though the practice of piety originated in Spain, the Filipinos have added local color and character to it. Chapter 3 focuses on the veneration of Santo Niño of Cebu, and of the suffering Christ, and devotion to Our Lady of Perpetual Help, noting that these popular pieties have the seal of church approval. Devotion to the Blessed Virgin Mary is especially strong due to Filipinos' high esteem for mothers. This chapter deliberates that in spite of anti-colonial sentiments among many Asians, Catholicism has flourished on Filipino soil.

Accommodation and inculturation are important themes because religious practice is rooted in every cultural framework. Chapter 4 evaluates Matteo Ricci's effort to accommodate Confucianism with Christianity in China, thus laying the foundation for interreligious dialogue and establishing a bridge between the East and the West. Ricci firmly believed that Confucius's teaching on veneration of ancestors had nothing to do with superstitious beliefs, but rather is part and parcel of Chinese social and cultural life. Clearly, Chinese "popular religiosity" has the linguistic and ritual resources that can be accommodated into the liturgy. For example, in Hong Kong, Catholic funeral rites include bowing three times in front of the altar and encoffining in the presence of the priest and family members before the start of the funeral service.

The practice of inculturation also brings risks when there is a tendency for popular religion to operate outside the jurisdiction of ecclesiastical authorities. The church is concerned that some of the apparent Christian devotions could degenerate into superstitious beliefs, or worse, into some form of idolatry. Popular piety touches the heart more than the head, appealing to our emotions and our need for tangible results. Doctrines are important for the faith; however, people have the desire to experience the power of the Holy Spirit in their lives. Chapter 5 offers explanations on the important points in the *Directory on Popular Piety and the Liturgy*, issued by the Congregation for Divine Worship and the Discipline of the Sacraments in 2001. While acknowledging the church's need to control and guide the faithful in their spiritual life, this chapter also explores the fine line between superstition and piety, and the Rites Controversy, which centered on the Chinese cult of ancestor veneration.

Since 1981, the numbers of pilgrims going to Medjugorje, a small mountain village in Eastern Europe, has been increasing. From Hong Kong alone, a city where Catholics are a minority, at least two trips to this

Introduction

European village are organized every year. Some Catholics in the territory have been to Medjugorje at least three times. Many have admitted that they did not see an apparition of Our Lady; however, they have experienced a profound conversion in their lives. Chapter 7 discusses the historical background of this Marian apparition, and the Virgin's call for conversion in a world torn by political, cultural, and religious conflicts.

Since the seventeenth century, the church has promoted devotion to the Sacred Heart of Jesus through Margaret Alacoque to halt the spread of Protestantism, communism, and liberalism. In recent decades, devotion to the Sacred Heart has experienced a decline and has been replaced by devotion to the Divine Mercy, which has an ecumenical dimension as well. Chapter 6 compares and contrasts these two popular pieties, which have served the faithful at different times in history, by exploring the two forms of devotion from historical and theological perspectives. Although devotion to the Sacred Heart and devotion to the Divine Mercy are distinctive, they cannot be separated—it is the same Jesus that the faithful adore and venerate.

Participation in pilgrimages is immensely popular in Hong Kong. Most parishes organize trips to the Holy Land, Marian shrines, the sites of Martyrs in Nagasaki, and churches in Vietnam, Taiwan, and even Singapore. This is a result of social change and improvement of people's standard of living, further facilitated by inexpensive flights and well-organized tours accompanied by spiritual directors. In the conclusion of this work, we consider the universal experience of pilgrimages, and the importance given to sacred sites, apparitions, and visions. Many people have returned from pilgrimages spiritually renewed and charged.

Chapter 1

Popular Piety

> Now faith is the substance of things hoped for,
> the evidence of things not seen.
>
> —Heb 11:1

Strengthening one's faith through public acts of devotion creates hope not just for the afterlife, but also for the immediate benefits on Earth. It transforms one's personal life, which in turn leads to a conscious demand for change in the community where one lives. Among the poor and the disadvantaged, with hope comes courage and conviction to advance in their struggle against social injustice, material exploitation, and political oppression. Therefore popular piety can trigger political consciousness and mobilize action among the populace. Without this consciousness and liberative evangelization, popular religion may end up alienating the poor as well as deepening the status quo of the rich and the powerful.

This chapter discusses the positive and negative aspects of popular piety in the context of Latin America, demonstrating the connection between the practice of popular piety and the theology of liberation as espoused by Gustavo Gutiérrez. Purifying and renewing Catholicism through conscientization and liberative evangelization is an important countermeasure to minimize the negative impact of popular religion. In other words, the power of the gospel to transform people and society must be emphasized, especially since devotional practices are popular among the poor and marginalized. Being poor and having faith are potentialities that can motivate them to act, to fight for a more equitable society.

Defining Popular Piety

It is not possible to provide a precise definition of popular piety, which is seen as a chimera by scholars with different persuasions. At the same time, popular piety does not exist in the abstract. It is found in the concrete attitudes, beliefs, and practices of people in specific cultural and national contexts. Even within a country, there are differences. For example, in the Philippines, popular religion in Bicol province is different from those in Manila and Cebu. A description of popular religion should take into account historical, sociocultural, and political-economic factors. Religious practices are characterized as a people's way of "crying and remembering and aspiring," as in the words of Harvey Cox.[1] Popular piety represents the faith of the people "least integrated into the premises of modern society." However for someone like the Marxist Italian philosopher Antonio Gramsci, popular religion is essentially superstitious belief or folklore.

As mentioned earlier, I use the terms *popular piety, popular religion,* and *popular religiosity* interchangeably, and all within the Catholic context. Popular piety in the Catholic context is defined as the form of Christianity in which devotional practices such as praying the rosary, going on pilgrimages, and venerating the Virgin Mary and the saints, occupy a central position, while the sacramental life is relegated to the periphery.

Popular religion in Latin America is syncretic, a mixture of two religious legacies—pre-Christian indigenous religious beliefs and imported Iberian Catholicism. Leonardo Boff holds that "Catholicity as the synonym of universality is only possible and attainable through the process of syncretism from which catholicity itself results.[2]" Thus, according to Boff, the poor and marginalized, those who live their faith together with other religious expressions and understand Catholicism as a living reality, are open to changes from other elements. They view syncretism as a normal, natural process. On the contrary, for those who reside in the privileged position in the Catholic institution, syncretism is a threat that must be avoided at all cost.

---

1. Cox, *The Seduction of the Spirit*, 117.
2. Boff, *Church*, 89.

Characterized by economic, social, and cultural marginality, popular piety is often associated with underdevelopment and backwardness. To the Church, popular religiosity is sometimes considered a deviant form of Christianity that is cut off from its official liturgy. At the Medellín Conference (1968), however, the bishops generally agreed that there is no real break, but rather a continuum between popular religion and official Catholicism, differentiated only by a matter of degree. The people thus need to be catechized properly so that they are able to see the coexistence and harmony of popular piety and the official Church liturgy.

Positive and Negative Aspects

Perhaps it is easier to understand popular piety by underscoring its strengths and weaknesses rather than trying to define it. The *Directory on Popular Piety and the Liturgy* considers popular piety as a "true treasure of the people of God" because it manifests a real thirst for God, his presence and mercy. It develops "Christian resignation in the face of irremediable situations" (*Directory* 61),[3] and helps the faithful to bear suffering patiently, to have a measure of detachment from material things, and to be in solidarity with others.

In its authentic forms, popular piety allows the gospel to express local cultural forms and values, with the message of salvation and the freedom that Christ won for us, which includes liberation from oppressions and exploitations. When there is a lack of pastoral care, popular piety can be a means to preserve the faith and promote fidelity to the message of Christ. It is the starting point to deepen our faith and bring it to maturity, a defense point to inspire evangelization and safeguard our faith from sectarian views.

The Church document *Evangelii Nuntiandi* presents a positive view of popular religion: "It manifests a thirst for God which only the simple and poor can know. It makes people capable of generosity and sacrifice even to the point of heroism, when it is a question of manifesting belief."[4] Influenced by this document, the Third Latin American Conference in Puebla, Mexico (January 1979) focused on the evangelization of culture in

---

3. All References here are taken from Congregation for Divine Worship and the Discipline of the Sacraments, *Directory on Popular Piety and the Liturgy*.

4. Pope Paul VI, *Evangelii Nuntiandi*, no. 48.

a vital way. They took the human person as the starting point to discuss the relationships between people among themselves and with God.

At Puebla, culture is defined as "the specific way in which human beings belonging to a given people cultivate their relationship with nature, with each other, and with God in order to arrive at an authentic and full humanity" (PD 386).[5] Evangelization here means conversion through the people's core values, which will in turn form a basis for the transformation of society. Such core values are related to how people affirm or reject God, which influence the way they understand the ultimate meaning of life. According to the Puebla document, evangelization is to take into account the whole human being.

Following this attitude, the Puebla Conference highlights the positive contributions of popular piety without dismissing its adverse effects. The Puebla Document regards popular piety as people's Catholicism that comprises "the whole complex of underlying beliefs rooted in God, the basic attitudes that flow from these beliefs, and the expressions that manifest them" (PD 444). Popular religion has thus left a profound influence on Latin American cultural identity. This *people's religion* is lived out in "a preferential way of the poor and simple" (PD 447). The religiosity of the people, the document asserts, is "a storehouse of values that offers the answers of Christian wisdom to the great questions of life" (PD 448). This Catholic wisdom of the people develops a vital synthesis, combining the divine and human, the spirit and body. It is a form of Christian humanism that affirms the dignity of the person, promotes solidarity, and teaches people how to live joyfully in the midst of difficulties and hardship.

Popular religion is not just an object of evangelization; it is also an active way in which the people evangelize themselves. The document also admits that popular religiosity has not been "sufficiently expressed in the organization of our societies and states" (PD 452). There are still "sinful structures" that widen the gap between the rich and the poor, perpetuate the menacing situations of injustices and humiliation faced by the poor and weakest. These structures radically contradict the values of personal dignity and human solidarity. In spite of this lamentable state of affairs, Latin American people carry the values of the gospel in their hearts, portending the potential to liberate them from the shackles of exploitations and oppressions.

---

5. All references here are taken from Eagleson and Scharper, eds., *Puebla and Beyond*.

Popular Piety

The Puebla Document presents the following positive elements of popular piety in the following:

1. Trinitarian presence in devotional practices
2. the mystery of incarnation and love of Mary
3. veneration of saints and remembrance of the dead
4. awareness of personal dignity and brotherhood
5. awareness of sin and the need to expiate it
6. ability to express faith in chant, image, gesture, color and dance, going beyond rationalism
7. ability to celebrate faith in expressive and communitarian forms
8. integration of the sacraments and sacramental into the people's lives
9. capacity for suffering and heroism, and profession of faith in times of trials and hardship
10. faith in the value of prayer and an acceptance of other people (PD 454).

The Puebla Document acknowledges aberrations of popular piety. Popular religiosity can lead to agnostic religious practices and political messianism, which are obstacles to evangelization (PD 456). Some are inherited, such as superstition, magic, fatalism, and idolatrous worship of power, fetishism, and ritualism. Other problems are due to lack of catechetical formation—static archaism, misinformation and ignorance, syncretic reinterpretation, and reduction of faith.

The Church's *Directory on Popular Piety and the Liturgy* therefore highlights the dangers of popular piety that are deficient of Christian elements, and the importance of belonging to the Church. Popular piety may place a disproportionate interest in saints, thereby neglecting the sovereignty of Christ as the source of our salvation in paschal mystery. Lack of direct contact with Scripture, isolation from the Church's sacramental life, excessive use of theatrical gestures, signs, and formulae are among the many pitfalls in practice. There is also a risk of promoting sects, superstitions, fatalism, and oppression (*Directory* 64).

One of the values highlighted by the *Directory* is Christian resignation in the face of irremediable situations. This resignation, however, can result in a fatalistic attitude, and not in line with the dynamic message of the gospel. In Latin America, Christianity has enabled people to endure the established social, political, and economic systems, however unjust these systems are. That is why Marx asserts that religion is the "*opium of the people*" and not "opium *for* the people," as amended by Lenin.[6]

Marx believed that religion "formulates alienation" for "it is the soul of alienation,"[7] asserting several forms of religious alienation. The first form is detachment from our "natural instincts." The second form is the "divine justification of social evil" by promising the poor and oppressed better things in the afterlife. Hence, heaven and hell are necessary to a society based on class; in a society without alienation, no one would need religion. Marx held that criticism of society starts with denunciation of religious or superstitious beliefs, and that revolution must overthrow religion because it is part of the evil social system. His description of religion as false consolation for the people provides a useful point of reference to discuss popular piety in relation to political liberation.

Popular Catholicism in Latin America encourages conformism and a passive mentality. In fact, teaching the people that "blessed are the poor" hardly ever transforms life. Catholicism has the tendency to stress a dualist view of reality, resulting in a religious attitude that is alienating to the poor. As such, popular religion in Latin America serves to reinforce the practices and rules of an unjust and oppressive social system. The influence of popular piety can make people feel inadequate and immature. Manifestation of popular piety is an expression of an alienated group, whose way of life is passive and lacks motivation to change their society for the better.[8] More importantly, this kind of popular piety is supported by the dominant structures to which the Church belongs.

Such religiosity discourages any move to change the structures of society. For example, an "order of creation" is used to justify the establishment; misery is theologically rationalized as "sin, indolence or laziness."[9] This conveys the message that this is the will of God, things have always been that way and will continue to be so. Such explanation puts a brake on initiatives for change. Pious exhortation is supposed to protect Christian values and defend the Christian way of life, though in reality, it serves as an ideological weapon of the rich against the poor.

---

6. Chadwick, *The Secularization of the European Mind*, 49.
7. Ibid., 64.
8. Bonino, "Popular Piety in Latin America," 152.
9. Ibid., 153.

Further, the ideology of peace at all costs and the Christian commandment of love have become an obstacle in the mobilization and transformation of society. The Church preaches against all forms of violence and insists on Christian charity: such exhortations are simply paralyzing given the situation in Latin America. José Míguéz Bonino maintains that Christian love can become an obstacle in not providing solidarity and support to people's struggle for justice and human rights.[10] Even the catechists in Bogota admit that popular piety is a hurdle to social transformation, especially when religious celebrations are commercialized and exploited by tourism.[11]

Popular religion is viewed as false praxis when it is disconnected from the consciousness and struggle of the poor. It leads to social apathy and promotes individualism, hindering people from revolutionary activities. Instead of taking personal responsibility, these people place all their trusts on miracles. Instead of struggling in solidarity with the poor, they seek benefits for themselves. Religious practice seems to separate people from "a true revolutionary praxis;"[12] popular piety that encourages social withdrawal and hope in the supernatural becomes an obstacle to liberation. This kind of popular religion or piety becomes mass religion, as suggested by Juan Luis Segundo.

Mass Religion

Segundo believes religion can have an "unsettling" effect on people unless they are secure enough to "disestablish" themselves.[13] These people will always be the minority because it is not easy to destroy a system and replace it with another. This means popular religion or "mass religion" will not be able to perform the function of changing people's mindset. However, Segundo admits that a religion that gives people psychological consolation can also be transformed into a revolutionary one. This can only happen when the existing reality has been transformed before a religious one can take place. The existing system must be a force that unsettles people before a religious revolution can take place. Without this initial process, popular religion cannot have the positive values and influence needed to transform society

---

10. Ibid., 154.
11. Candelaria, *Popular Religion and Liberation*, 5–6.
12. Ibid., 7.
13. Segundo, *Liberation of Theology*, 186.

for the better. In other words, economic, social, and political changes must take place before the religious structure can be transformed. We cannot assume that as popular religion forms part of the culture of the people, it will gradually evolve with the people.

Segundo does not believe the Church is capable of initiating the transformation process. In fact, he thinks the Church will be the last to change![14] Neither can the masses effect a change in society because their lives are tied into their traditional religious practices that have no relationship with their present roles in society. Mass religion or popular religion follow "*the line of least resistance.*"[15] With vested interests, the masses will not spend much energy or expenditure to transform society. The hope for Latin America, according to Segundo, is not to preserve their primitive culture, but to modernize and humanize their social structures. Only the minority of people from the educated Western middle class with a mature faith can assist in the liberation of society for the benefits of all. In other words, it would be the elites, with their knowledge and expertise, who can effect a transformation of society.

José Ortega y Gasset divides society into minorities and masses. The minorities are individuals or groups who are specially qualified. The mass is just an unsorted mass of people not specially qualified—"the average man"—one who is undifferentiated from another, "a generic type." The "minorities" do not think they are superior to the rest of the population—it means they tend to demand more of themselves, are willing to make sacrifices and are not afraid of difficulties and challenges. The masses, on the other hand, are characterized by inertia—like "mere buoys that float on the waves."[16] The select minorities are the movers and shakers in the community; they are activists, not conservatives or reactionaries. They are the ones who are capable of transforming society.

German philosopher Theodor Adorno is critical of popular culture, which is closely related to popular piety, because "the culture of the masses was a wholly synthetic concoction cynically imposed on them from above. Rather than cultural chaos or anarchy, the current situation was one of tight regimentation and control."[17] Adorno never doubts the top-down direction

14. Ibid., 201.
15. Ibid., 225.
16. Ortega y Gasset, *The Revolt of the Masses*, 13, 15.
17. Jay, *Adorno*, 119. Adorno was probably referring to the Nazi occupation in Europe between 1939 and 1945.

of cultural domination: it is never a culture that arises spontaneously from the bottom, like popular art, as we are led to believe. It is the elites that govern and give expression to a cultural phenomenon.

As we have seen, the danger of popular piety becoming a tool of oppression and alienation, giving people false hope and consolation, and inculcating superstitious beliefs, are prevalent in poor and developing countries. In Latin America, for instance, due to a lack of proper pastoral care, there are "signs of erosions and distortions. Aberrant substitutes and regressive form of syncretism have already surfaced" (PD 452). When religion is closed in upon itself; the belief that salvation is achieved merely by mechanical recitations, observing rites and norms, while the need for conversion is avoided. Boff writes: "The symbols do not give way to Mystery but [are an] idolatrous substitute for it, breaking it down to various mysteries. On the psychological level religion compensates for human frustrations and generates a false sense of security."[18] In regressive forms of syncretism, symbols are dignified as magical.

Evangelization vs. Oppression

It is thus of crucial importance to evangelize the people's religiosity by first appealing to the "Christian memory of our peoples," building on Latin America's 500 years of Christianity (PD 457). The pastoral pedagogy must be directed toward purifying and renewing Catholicism; Catholicism must be made more dynamic by the gospel message; catechists and pastors must know the symbols and nonverbal languages of the people so that effective dialogue can take place. The main objective is to make the people's religion more mature. Equally important is for the elites "to accept the spirit of their people, purify it, scrutinize it, and flesh it out in a prominent way" (PD 462), encouraging them to participate and contribute in the people's manifestation of their faith.

In this sense, the Puebla Document seeks to unite all people in Christian solidarity, rich and poor, literate and illiterate. Special pastoral attention must be directed toward the popular devotions of the natives or indigenous people so that faith may grow and be renewed without sacrificing cultural identity. The religiosity of the people must harmonize with the liturgy of the Church through cross-fertilization. Popular piety with its symbolic and expressive richness can infuse our liturgy with "creative

18. Boff, *Church*, 100.

dynamism" (PD 465). As "privileged locales" of evangelization, sanctuaries and shrines must be purified of commercialization and other forms of manipulation (PD 463).

The Puebla Document speaks of the two dimensions of liberation when connecting evangelization through the authentic realization of the human being. First, the liberation of the person from all forms of bondage: from personal and social sins, and from everything that destroys the individual and society. Second, the liberation in terms of progressive growth through communion with God and other human beings. This liberation is being realized in history, in our own personal lives, taking place in all the different dimensions of human existence. In this liberative process, economic, social, and cultural spheres must be transformed by the message of the gospel. The church is to safeguard this authentic form of liberation from manipulation by ideological systems and political parties (PD 482–83; EN 32), especially godless ideologies such as Marxism. At the same time, the Church also needs to discourage any use of violence and class struggle dialectics. The challenge of protecting against manipulation while encouraging progressive evangelization requires examining the relationship between popular piety and the theology of liberation.

There are scholars who think popular religion or popular piety is not "genuine" Christianity, which is supposed to be liberating. Yet, as discussed earlier, popular piety very often alienates the poor from critical consciousness about their exploitative situations. There is also economic and political manipulation of religious consciousness by domination and dependence. Segundo Galilea writes:

> In a two-sided process, popular religion at once made the oppressed find their situation of exploitation acceptable through its symbolic structure (of evasion and resignation), which was fomented by the dominant culture and the ruling class, and at the same time injected the ideology of these ruling classes into the consciousness of the people, thereby reinforcing their dependence on the secular level.[19]

Even the Church's *Directory on Popular Piety and the Liturgy* speaks of "Christian resignation in the face of irremediable situations," thus unwittingly reinforcing the dominant ideology and status quo of the rich and powerful. Popular piety is looked upon as a deviant Christianity, thus incompatible with liberation theology.

19. Galilea, "The Theology of Liberation," 42.

Regarding the criticism of popular religion as a distorted or ideologized Christianity, it is argued that there is no such thing as "pure" Christianity. The faith has always had to be expressed through a particular cultural medium. While there are ambiguities and weaknesses in popular religion, such as the case in Latin America, the same can also be said of other forms of cultural Catholicism. Liberation can be achieved by uniting the struggle for social justice with the consciousness of one's own culture, which includes popular or folk religion. In Latin America, the culture is Christian, therefore it has liberating potentials.

Oppression and piety are related, according to Gustavo Gutiérrez. The exploited are both poor and believing, representing two potentials in the people.[20] In fact, popular religion or Catholicism in Latin America forms part of the identity of the people. In many aspects, it is the most "creative and original part of the people's heritage."[21]

Since popular religion is very much part of Latin American cultural phenomenon, Aldo Büntig maintains that "there is a pressing and immediate need to situate and integrate the popularized Catholicism, which is rooted in the very depths of our people, within the irrepressible process through which our continent is now living."[22] It seems that religion, rather than politics, is the only thing that people feel deeply. Thus "we must *start from* the reality of the people, including their way of internalizing and expressing the religious element."[23] By "people," Büntig identifies those individuals who are deeply aware of the injustice that is prevalent in their society and struggle to change it. These individuals possess both "*sacral and non sacral*" Christian values that must be cultivated.[24] Hence, pastoral effort must lead people to participate in an active way toward their liberation.

Popular religion is also potentially valuable in raising political consciousness and mobilizing the people. It is important that the revolutionary power of the oppressed class be cultivated and organized. The belief of the people, this believing dimension of the masses, must be developed and directed by selected qualified Christian leaders and activists.

Segundo and Ortega y Gasset rightly assert that only that a select minority, and not the masses, has the capability and will to effect change in

20. Gutiérrez, *The Power of the Poor in History*, 97.
21. Galilea, "The Theology of Liberation," 43.
22. Segundo, *Liberation of Theology*, 197.
23. Ibid., 197–98.
24. Ibid., 198.

society. In the context of popular piety and liberation theology, only the competent and committed Christian activists can make a difference to the lives of the people living in poverty and misery. Theologians and Church authorities generally agree that popular religion has within itself the seed of dynamic spirituality, but it must be cultivated by conscientization and liberative evangelization, led by the dedicated few.

Conscientization, grounded in Marxist political consciousness, means "going beyond the spontaneous phase of apprehension of reality to a critical phase," according to Paolo Freire. This occurs when reality becomes a knowable object. The more a person conscientizes himself, the more he is able to pierce though reality and grasp the essence of the object before him, and to analyze it. Conscientization is also a "commitment in time," "historical awareness," and "critical insertion into history." Human beings thus are called upon to be responsible for their own lives by directing their own destiny. "The more they are conscientized, the more they exist."[25]

According to Paolo Freire, conscientization occurs when I realize that I am oppressed, and will liberate myself by attempting to change the concrete situation where I find myself alienated. Further, Freire maintains that we must adopt a utopian attitude toward the world when we conscientize. In fact, we must conscientize ourselves into "a Utopian agent."[26] To be utopian agents is to denounce the dehumanizing structure in our society and at the same time to announce the structure that humanizes our society. Utopian agents are prophetic and hopeful as Freire sees great possibility for constructing a utopian theology of hope: "The Utopian posture of the denouncing, announcing, historically committed Christians who are convinced that the historical vocation of men is not to adapt, not to bend pressures, not to spend 90 per cent of their time making concessions in order to salvage what we call the historical vocation of the Church."[27]

The process of conscientization forces us to make a decision, to be on the side of the poor and oppressed. Conscientization reveals to us that God wants us to act. Freire claims that conscientization demands an Easter: We must die to be born again. Every Christian must live his Easter, which is his utopia.[28]

---

25. Freire, "Conscientisation," 25.
26. Ibid.
27. Ibid., 26.
28. Ibid., 30.

Popular Piety

Gustavo Gutiérrez adds that such a concept of utopia helps us understand the relation between faith and politics based on its relationship with a historical situation. According to Gutiérrez, the process of liberation is a complex process with various levels of meaning. First, there is economic, social, and political liberation, corresponding to the level of scientific rationality. Second, there is the liberation that leads to the creation of a just and peaceful society where human beings live in solidarity with one another, corresponding to the idea of utopia. Third, there is the liberation from sin, which leads to communion with God and with one another. This corresponds to the level of faith.[29] Gutiérrez is aware that faith and political action alone will not be able to succeed in the liberation process unless there is an effort to create a new type of person in a different society, which he characterized as utopia. This utopia provides the basis for the struggle for better living conditions. A political path is valid when it moves toward the "utopia of a freer, more human humankind, the protagonist of its own history."[30] Utopia, far from making political activists idealistic and dreamy, helps them to be realistic and to focus on their goal, which is to achieve social equality in society. The loss of utopia leads to "bureaucratism and sectarianism" in new structures, which oppress humanity.[31]

Thus, utopia and political struggle for a more equitable society should go hand in hand. Creative imagination and concrete historical actions are needed for the transformation of society into an equitable one. Gutiérrez explains: "Political dogmatism is as worthless as religious dogmatism; both represent a step backward toward ideology. But for utopia validly to fulfill this role, it must be verified in social praxis; it must become effective commitment, without intellectual purisms, without inordinate claims; it must be revised and concretized constantly."[32]

In practical terms, the utopia of liberation means the creation of new social consciousness where the means of production and political process are transformed for the benefit of the poor and dispossessed. Utopia leads to a *cultural revolution*, which is the creation of a new humanity characterized by solidarity and by communion with God. This implies the liberation from sin that, in Gutiérrez's opinion, is the root of all injustice and exploitation.

---

29. Gutiérrez, *A Theology of Liberation*, 137.
30. Ibid., 138.
31. Ibid.
32. Ibid., 139.

Faith gives us hope that the abolition of exploitation is possible with God's help: "Faith reveals to us the deep meaning of the history which we fashion with our own hands: it teaches us that every human act which is oriented toward the construction of a more just society has value in terms of communion with God."[33] Hence, an unjust society is against the will of God. Gutiérrez reminds us that the gospel does not provide a utopia, it is our responsibility to create one with the help of God. We need to play our part in the process of liberation, and in playing our part to promote justice, we are to discover God.

So far we have discussed the importance of conscientization and its relationship with utopia. Only when the poor are conscientized and understand that the abolition of unjust structures is possible (in other words, utopia is not merely an ideal but a concept that can be realized) can they emerge as a forceful presence to change the course of history. This issue of conscientization is an important step in liberation theology because the poor may not even realize that they are being victimized: "From capitalism to colonialism, imperialism, globalism, or consumerism, the capitalists have been clever in shifting the sufferings to the working people that working people may not even realize the problem."[34] Only when the poor are conscientized can they then make their presence felt.

The Puebla Document emphasizes the urgent need to liberate people from "the idol of absolutized power" so that they may live in a society that is just and free. Latin America needs a political order that will respect human dignity and promote peace and harmony in the community. The Puebla Document emphasizes equality for all citizens, the right to exercise their freedoms and self-determination for the peoples, and the urgent need to re-establish justice (PD 502–6). To perform this task there must be institutions that are operative and administered by honest and capable people. For the Church, this requires a new perspective in theologizing. For Gutiérrez, it is an attempt to find ways of living the faith in "new social-cultural categories" which involves rereading the gospel message in the light of liberation praxis.[35]

This rereading of the gospel is carried out in view of a proclamation of God's words which must always take place within the Christian community, the *ecclesia*, in solidarity with the poor and exploited classes. In

---

33. Ibid.
34. Li and Rowland, "Hope," 186.
35. Gutiérrez, *The Power of the Poor in History*, 66.

this process of reformulation of the gospel message, we encounter a new "political dimension" of God's message.[36] When we read the gospel in this manner, we need to take a political stand; we cannot remain neutral or apolitical. In fact, the gospel message itself is political by nature and we are asked to make a decision, to be or not to be, for Christ.

The gospel calls us to action, to do the will of the Father in heaven (Matt 7:21). This is a fight against injustice and exploitation, to create a more humane, compassionate society, and a proclamation of God who loves all men and women in a society marred by extreme injustice and oppression. Such proclamation is bound to create conflicts—"the political dimension comes to light in the very dynamism of a word that seeks to be incarnate in history."[37] The poor and the oppressed will come to a deep realization and understanding of the unjust structures which they have come to accept as "normal." With this new consciousness, they will be empowered to enter directly into the political arena to fight for a more equitable society.

In Gutiérrez's opinion, this is political reductionism only if the gospel is placed at the service of the rich and powerful. It is not political reductionism if, in solidarity with the poor, we denounce this manipulation of the gospel by the exploiters. Christ's liberating message cannot be reduced to just a "religious message" which has nothing to do with the concrete historical existence. The liberation by Christ is total—it involves the transformation of our social, economic and political situation—so that men and women live in peace and with dignity. Gutiérrez further states that this is fully understood only when "this liberation leads this same history out beyond itself, to a fullness that transcends the scope of all human doing or telling."[38] The gospel message cannot be identified with any political or social system—the Word of God is a clarion call to every historical situation to proclaim Christ as liberator and Lord of history in the concrete sense.

Toward a Theology of Liberation

Liberation theology, according to Gustavo Gutiérrez, is a commitment and commentary of Christian communities, groups of people who are becoming more aware of the oppression and exploitation that they are suffering and which they see as incompatible with their faith. It is the concrete life

36. Ibid., 67.
37. Ibid., 68.
38. Ibid., 69.

experiences that give this theology its special character. Faith and life are intrinsically linked together and the unity gives this theology "its prophetic vigor and its potentialities."[39] In fact, theology should not be confined to abstract and timeless truths because "faith means not only truths to be affirmed, but also an existential stance, an attitude, a commitment to God and to human beings."[40]

If faith is a commitment to God and to human beings, it implies also a commitment to the process of liberation. The Second Vatican Council regards this process as "a sign of the times." It is first of all a call to action, and then a call to interpretation. The process of liberation is the sign of the times and a call to action. To do this properly, Gutiérrez suggests utilizing the social sciences for a more accurate understanding of the Latin American situation.

The theology of liberation is, in practice, the theology of salvation. The gospel is fundamentally a message of salvation, which is related to the construction of this world. Gutiérrez insists there is a relationship between the kingdom of God and human work. Hegel, the German philosopher, helps us understand our times by holding that the human person is the agent of history and that history is nothing else than the process of human liberation. "Since it is a history of human emancipation, the human being creates history by self-liberation. To liberate oneself, to emancipate oneself, is to create history."[41] With this understanding of Hegel, Gutiérrez speaks of "human liberation, of human emancipation throughout history, which will pass through radical social change, revolution, and even beyond these." Gutiérrez further explains the dimension of faith being: "It is not merely a matter of knowing the meaning of earthly action, but of knowing the meaning of human liberation in the perspective of faith, and what faith can say not only to human action in this world but to human liberation."[42]

Gutiérrez maintains that theologians must see the need for human liberation, a sign of the times, and scrutinize it carefully. This reading and observation of the sign of the times will give us a better perspective in judging economic and political dominations which not only imprison people but also prevent them from being human. Gutiérrez laments that Christians

---

39. Gutiérrez, *A Theology of Liberation*, xix. Some material in this chapter appeared in Mong, *A Tale of Two Theologians*, 17–21; 32–36.

40. Gutiérrez, "Toward a Theology of Liberation," 63.

41. Ibid., 67–68.

42. Ibid., 68.

have not really understood the real meaning of *Populorum Progressio*, the encyclical of Pope Paul VI on the development of peoples, when they focus more on sacraments and grace than on the "global vision of humanity."[43] He urges us to focus more on a God who is present in this world than on one who is located outside of this world. He agrees with Karl Barth that "From the moment God became man, the human being is the measure of all things."[44] Thus the work of constructing and developing the world has salvific value. In fact, everything that contributes to growth in humanity has salvific value. In other words "integral development"[45] is salvation.

Salvation is not limited to religious or spiritual realities and values. It must be understood as the transformation of human beings—"from less human conditions to more human conditions." In the biblical sense, it is the freedom of captives and the oppressed, liberation from slavery. The coming of the messiah brings about the deliverance from oppression. The coming of the kingdom of God is associated with better living conditions for human beings. Thus as Christians we must struggle for a more equitable world by getting rid of servitude, slavery, and oppression, indicating a close connection exists between the kingdom and the elimination of poverty and misery. "The kingdom comes to suppress injustice."[46] Hence we can say the theology of liberation is the theology of salvation.

Following the teaching of Vatican II, Gutiérrez asserts that history is one and we encounter God in history: "The Lord is the goal of human history, the focal point of the longings of history and of civilization, the center of the human race, the joy of every heart and the answer to all its yearnings."[47] Gutiérrez holds that "if there is a finality inscribed in history, then the essence of Christian faith is to believe in Christ, that is, to believe that God is irreversibly committed to human history."[48] In Christ, we see the human face of God. Thus, if you gave food and drink to anyone in need, you have given it to Christ (Matt 25:45).

Gutiérrez speaks of the *irruption of the poor*, which means that in the past, the poor were voiceless, but now they have the opportunity to express themselves concerning their own subjugation and suffering. This *new*

---

43. Ibid.
44. Ibid., 69.
45. Ibid., 70.
46. Ibid., 73.
47. Pope Paul VI, *Gaudium et spes*, no. 45.
48. Gutiérrez, "Toward a Theology of Liberation," 74.

presence of the poor is not confined to Latin America, but has spread to Africa and Asia, and to minorities living in both rich and poor nations. This new presence also includes women, who were neglected in the past and were described as "doubly oppressed and marginalized" among the poor of Latin America.[49]

For Gutiérrez, liberation is intrinsically tied to this new presence of the poor who in the past were "absent from our history."[50] Liberation theology strives to empower them to direct their own lives and to change the course of their destiny from bondage to freedom. Liberation theology enables the poor "to think out their own faith."[51] It seeks to interpret the signs of the times by reflecting on it critically in the light of the gospel.

As we review the situations in the countries mentioned above, the Church has the responsibility and obligation to fight for the rights of the poor, which includes "dominated peoples" or "non-persons," minorities, and women. Our attention must be to the poor first without excluding others. The church has to exercise a "preferential option for the poor," an "option" that we have the freedom to commit ourselves to the care of the poor first. Unfortunately, the Christianization of Latin America has been carried out at immense human cost—the massacre of native peoples and the destruction of their cultures. It is time for the Church to repent and make recompense by giving priority to the poor.

As discussed earlier, most poor people are pious and devout. Being poor and believing are qualities that the gospel has highlighted . . . for example, in Latin America, popular Catholicism is part of their identity. Led by enlightened Church leaders, the faith of the poor has the potentiality to transform society for the better. Thus, pastoral activities must help raise the consciousness of the poor and encourage them to participate actively in their struggle for greater justice, more equality, and freedom from exploitation and oppression by the rich and powerful. The practice of popular piety, infused with the dynamics of the gospel message, can help to raise political awareness, a sense of responsibilities, and promote solidarity. The faith of the poor has an immense potential for the transformation of individual lives as well as the society as a whole.

The theology of liberation is still relevant because *the poor you will always have with you* (Matt 26:11) and for most of them the practice of

---

49. Gutiérrez, *A Theology of Liberation*, xx.
50. Ibid., xxi.
51. Ibid.

popular religion is the way they express their faith and cope with the harsh realities of life. Popular piety can be a powerful tool to bring down the mighty from their seats and exalt those of low degree (Luke 1:52). This is also the message revealed by the apparition of the Virgin of Guadalupe to Juan Diego, which will be the focus in the following chapter.

Chapter 2

Our Lady of Guadalupe

The arrival of the Spanish in the Americas was a visitation, a special dispensation of either divine favor or wrath, as defined in the Merriam-Webster dictionary. The initial impression of the natives was divine favor—the gods had favored them with a visit from on high. It turned out to be a terrible kind of divine "wrath" as the Spanish brought with them mass destruction, diseases, and general genocide. Following timorously in the footsteps of the so-called conquistador or "conquering" soldiers were the priests who attempted to convert the remnants to the Catholic faith. In Mexico, one of the earliest civilizations to be destroyed by the Spanish, the spread and acceptance of the Catholic faith was coincidentally aided by the phenomenon of Our Lady of Guadalupe.

This miraculous event had now passed into the collective consciousness of the Mexican people, and is regarded by many as a binding force of the nation's cultural identity: *Somos Mexicanos, Somos Gaudalupanos*. In other words, the devotion to the Virgin of Guadalupe is part of Mexican national consciousness. In the apparition, the Virgin offered her message of faith, hope, and love, out of the crazed massacre of the natives by the same people who carried the crucifix and the gun.

According to tradition, the Blessed Virgin Mary appeared to a newly baptized Catholic, Juan Diego, at the hill of Tepeyac, north of Mexico City, in December 1531. The Virgin directed Juan Diego, a native Indian, to Juan de Zumárraga, the bishop-elect of Mexico, a Spanish Franciscan, and instructed him to have a church built on the site where she appeared. Turned down by Zumárraga, Juan Diego reported to the Virgin about the failure of his mission. But the Virgin told him to return to the bishop the following day. This time the bishop asked for a sign to confirm the truth of the apparition.

While returning home, Juan Diego learned that his uncle, Juan Bernardino, was dying of the plague. The following day, Diego rushed to search for a priest to anoint his uncle and attempted to avoid meeting the Virgin at Tepeyac. But she found him and told him that his uncle was cured. The Virgin then directed him to a hill where he collected flowers that were blooming when the weather was cold and the soil was barren. Juan Diego folded the flowers in his cloak made of cactus fibers called *tilma*. In the presence of the bishop, Juan Diego opened the *tilma* and the flowers fell to the floor. Imprinted on his *tilma* was the image of the Virgin Mary. The bishop-elect begged for forgiveness for his skepticism, then adored and displayed the image in a public place till a small church at Tepeyac, now called Guadalupe, was constructed to hold the sacred image.[1]

This chapter discusses the significance of the Our Lady of Guadalupe phenomenon, with an examination of the historical context in which the apparition took place, the various interpretations of this event, and the controversies surrounding it. This chapter attempts to demonstrate that the conquest of Mexico was just as tragic and brutal because the conquistadors attempted not only to destroy the Aztec empire physically, but its cultural and spiritual heritage as well. A model of inculturation, devotion to Our Lady of Guadalupe symbolizes a religious triumph of the indigenous people as they responded and adopted the conquistadors' faith as their own, but with native characteristics. The name "Guadalupe" was appropriated from a place in Extremadura, Spain, and though not part of the natives' vocabulary, Guadalupe became an emblem that brought together the various disparate groups in Mexican society, forging a national identity that is cohesive and enduring.

The military campaign of the soldier of fortune Hernán Cortés brought about the conquest of Mexico by forces of arms, but the spiritual conquest of Mexico was accomplished by the gentler power of the Blessed Virgin Mary. The conquistadors overran the old, vibrant Aztec empire, but the Virgin is said to have captured the hearts of the native population. Let us examine the religious practice of the Aztec empire before the arrival of the Spaniards in sixteenth century.

1. Valeriano, "Nican Mopohua." The *Nican Mapohua* is an account the apparition of Our Lady of Guadalupe written in the language and style of the Nahua poets with its emphasis on the visual imagery, sound, and symbolic meaning. Some material in this chapter appears in Mong, "Our Lady of Guadalupe."

Aztec culture

Aztecs were the Nahuatl-speaking people who ruled central and southern Mexico during the fifteenth and early sixteenth centuries. The Aztec people were successful in creating a state and later an empire due to their remarkable system of agriculture, intensive cultivation of all available land, and elaborate systems of irrigation and reclamation of swampland. They became a rich, populous state as the result of their advanced technique in agriculture and irrigation.[2]

Under the ruler Itzcóatl (1428–40), Tenochtitlán, the Aztec ancient capital, formed alliances with the neighboring states of Texcoco and Tlacopan, and became the dominant power in central Mexico. Through commerce and conquest, Tenochtitlán came to establish an empire of 400 to 500 states with about five or six million people by 1519. It was the most densely populated settlement in that part of the world at that time. The Aztec state was essentially despotic, in which the military played a prominent role. The priestly and bureaucratic classes also took part in the administration of the empire. At the bottom of the heap were the serfs, indentured servants, and slaves.[3]

Syncretistic, the Atzec religion absorbed elements from its neighboring cultures in Mesoamerica. In the Aztec pantheon of deities were the following: Huitzilopochtli, god of war; Tonatiuh, god of the sun; Tlaloc, god of rain; and Quetzalcóatl, the Feathered Serpent, who was part deity and part culture hero. Human sacrifice was a common practice. Thus in every Aztec city and large town, there was a large central square where a high pyramidal temple rose. In the temple, the sacrificial victims climbed the steps to the platform at the top, bent backward over a large convex slab of polished stone, and a priest would tear the victim's heart out with an immense knife for all to see. The Aztecs practiced cannibalism by eating the limbs of the sacrificial victims. It has been reported that at least 50,000 human sacrifices were performed annually to appease the gods.[4]

Aztec wars provided sacrificial victims, whose blood and hearts were fed to the gods. Appeased, the gods would provide sun, rain, crops, and all the necessities of life. Huitzilopochtili, the Aztec god of war and sun, required an enormous amount of human blood and hearts, so that he could

---

2. "Aztec," https://www.britannica.com/topic/Aztec.
3. Ibid.
4. Carroll, *Our Lady of Guadalupe and the Conquest of Darkness*, 8.

provide protection for his people. Without such nourishments, the Indians feared that they would lose their battle against the forces of that were against them, such as drought, famine, and defeat in wars. There is evidence that before the Spanish conquest, there was a growing discontent among the population because the Aztec priests were demanding too many human sacrifices. Nonetheless, the people continued to believe human sacrifices were necessary for the preservation of their way of life and also the cosmic order.[5]

Warren Carroll, a convert to Roman Catholicism and founder of Christendom College in the United States in 1977, interpreted the religion of the Aztec as devil worship: "Nowhere else in human history has Satan so formalized and institutionalized his worship with so many of his own actual titles and symbols."[6] Carroll thus viewed the Spanish conquest and the coming of Christianity into the Americas, in particular, the apparition of Our Lady of Guadalupe, as the triumph of good over evil—the conquest of darkness. Carroll is also aware that the motivation behind the Spanish conquest of Mexico was not altogether religious or noble, let alone altruistic. Many Spanish conquistadors were purely motivated by greed for gold. Here is an Aztec's graphic description of the Spaniards' avarice and lust for gold:

> And when they were given those presents [gold], the Spaniards burst into smiles, their eyes shone with pleasure; they were delighted by them. They picked up the gold and fingered it like monkeys; they seemed to be transported by joy, as if their hearts were illumined and made new. The truth is that they [Spaniards] longed and lusted for gold. Their bodies swelled with greed, and their hunger was ravenous; they hungered it like pigs for that gold.[7]

The Aztec rulers thought that the Spaniards would be contented with the gold they received as gifts, but these presents only increased their avarice. Thus, driven by the desire for gold, glory for Spain, and perhaps also to spread the gospel as a kind of spiritual conquest, the Spanish conquistador, Hernán Cortés, took Emperor Montezuma II (reigned 1502–20) as prisoner; he later died in custody. Montezuma's successors, Cuitláhuac and

---

5. Madsen, "Religious Syncretism," 370.

6. Carroll, *Our Lady of Guadalupe and the Conquest of Darkness*, 9.

7. Leon-Portilla, ed., *The Broken Spears*, 51. The Aztecs valued brightly colored feathers more than gold and sliver.

Cuauhtémoc, were no match for the Spaniard forces that captured Tenochtitlán in 1521. Thus ended the Aztec empire.[8]

Clash of Civilizations

The Aztec empire and the Spanish nation were more than a world apart. While the nobility and common people of Aztec society were conditioned to think and act collectively, the Spaniards were individualists to the core, pledging obedience only to their monarchs and the Church. The population in the Aztec empire was held in thrall by fear and horror as we can imagine with such human sacrifices occurring so often, whereas the Spaniard explorers and soldiers during the fifteenth century were a tough and fearless people. They were locked in mortal combat with both neighboring Portugal and France, and with Moorish forces that had occupied Iberia for more than 770 years.[9] Troops of King Ferdinand and Queen Isabella completed the Reconquista or Re-conquest of Spain in 1492, soon to be followed by the discovery of the New World. Years of intense struggle and hardship had transformed the Spaniards into a warlike race quite like the militant Aztec in this respect.

The violence institutionalized in Aztec religious practice was well matched by the Spanish justice system implemented in New Spain with its severe punishments and harsh penitential practices. Both cultures were violent in different ways: "The mutual scandal of both was on the issue of human life. The Iberians were scandalized at the Nahua for practicing human sacrifice and the Nahua were scandalized at the Iberians [Spaniards] who had so little respect for life that they easily killed, even over a game of dice!"[10]

Conquest of Mexico

A number of factors facilitate the Spanish conquest of Mexico. First, there was certain unrest among the Nahuatl population. "Nahuatl" refers to the people living in central Mexico. The Aztecs were a demographic sub-group of the Nahuatl that dominated the rest of the group. An indigenous military

---

8. "Aztec," https://www.britannica.com/topic/Aztec.
9. Carroll, *Our Lady of Guadalupe and the Conquest of Darkness*, 12.
10. Elizondo, "Evangelization Is Inculturation," 20.

group, the Aztecs developed an aristocracy that exploited and oppressed the rest of the population. Naturally, with their obsession with human sacrifices, the Aztecs were hated and feared by the rest of the subordinate groups. The arrival of the Spaniards thus represented a potential for liberation for these suppressed and exploited non-Aztecs. In fact, the Aztec had totally perverted the religion of the people with their lust for human sacrifices.[11]

Second, the Spanish conquest coincided with the ancient Nahuatl predictions that their civilization would come to an end. They predicted that the god Quetzalcóatl would return from the east. He was supposed to be a big man, with blue eyes and blond hair—the Spaniard, Hernán Cortés, fit that description. Thus the natives believed that the Spaniards would come and redeem them from the cruelty of the Aztecs.[12] Unfortunately, the Spanish conquistadors proved to be just as cruel and savage as the Aztecs. In fact, the Spaniards were worse than the Aztec rulers, as we shall discover. A stratified colonial society was established in Mexico with the conquistadors as the privileged and ruling class, and the rest of the indigenous population as servants. The poor natives thus replaced one despotic and exploitative regime with another one.

Another tragic scenario was that endemic diseases brought by the Europeans killed many indigenous people—many died of smallpox, typhoid fever, measles, and diphtheria epidemics. Since they were isolated from the rest of the world, the natives had not developed any resistance to such diseases. Other factors that helped the Spaniards to crush the Aztecs were superior arms, Spain expansionist policy, and the desire to spread Christianity. Some Spaniards truly believed God sanctioned their conquest and the subjugation of the natives.[13] Greed and the lust for gold made the Spaniards ruthless, violent, and cruel. The live burning of their enemies by the Spanish conquistadors was just as horrifying as Aztec human sacrifices.

Regarding the actual war against the natives, historian Burr C. Brundage writes: "The siege of the city of Mexico is one of the most savage and desperate encounters in all history." One native eyewitness remembered, "In the streets lay broken bones and torn out hanks of hair. Houses had fallen apart; they lay open with their walls spattered with blood. Worms wriggled in the cluttered streets. Walls were dirtied with bits of brains. The

---

11. Rodriquez, *Our Lady of Guadalupe*, 2.
12. Ibid., 3.
13. Ibid.

water was dyed with blood. Even so we drank it. We drank it with salty blood."[14] It was a war calculated by the Spaniards to bring terror and total destruction of the city. Many Indians and their close allies were killed, drowned, or died from disease or starvation.

The result of this clash of civilizations was the destruction of the Nahuatl and their way of life. Even the Spanish clergy, in their enthusiasm to convert the indigenous people to Christianity, "lost their humanity even as they pursued divinity."[15] While Warren Carroll highlights the human sacrifices of the Aztecs, Rodriguez reminds us of the physical violence that the Spaniards inflected on the natives. Local paintings depict Spanish dismembering Aztecs and eyewitness records widespread physical and sexual abuse of indigenous women. Under the First Audience, leader of the Spanish civil governing body, Nuño de Guzman, natives were enslaved, children sold, women violated, the clergy threatened, and dissenters killed.[16] His profit-seeking regime was one of sheer brutalities, cruelties, and violence.

The spiritual devastation brought about by Spanish conquest was even more traumatic for the Aztec people—it was difficult for the natives to accept the religion of the Spaniards who were violent and cruel even though some of the missionaries were meek and gentle. It must have been confusing for the natives to find that both the saintly Franciscan friars and the evil conquistadors shared the same religious and cultural identities. Warren Carroll, in his book *Our Lady of Guadalupe and the Conquest of Darkness*, highlights the natives' enthusiasm for baptism but it was more likely that most of the natives were forced to abandon their ancient religion.

When challenged by Christian missionaries, the Aztec priests did not appeal to any theological explanation, but to tradition itself. For the Aztec, the wisdom of the past was rooted in the present, in the continuation of their tradition. When human sacrifices were prohibited, the Aztec priests were completely lost for they thought that their gods had died too. The natives experienced a crisis of faith and some committed suicide.[17] Elizondo writes:

> At the level of rational discourse, the missioners prepared a very clear and concise evangelization program, but they were no match for the Nahua theologians. In the *Coloquios de los Doce* the Nahuas

---

14. Brundage, *A Rain of Darts*, 285–86.
15. Rodriquez, *Our Lady of Guadalupe*, 10.
16. Anderson and Chávez, *Our Lady of Guadalupe*, 71.
17. Ibid., 75–76.

completely countered the argument of the theologians with their own arguments. In the end the final argument of the missioners was, "You have to accept that our God defeated yours in battle!"[18]

Thus it was not surprising that the Aztecs resented Christianity—it was a "direct conflict between native polytheism and Christian monotheism."[19] While some friars tried to learn the Nahuatl language and culture, most were ignorant, and believed they were bringing a more civilized way of life to the native population. Some Spanish even questioned, "Do the Indians have a soul?" Since they doubted if the natives possessed a soul, it was likely that the Spaniards would treat them like beasts of burden. The conquest of Mexico can be interpreted as a successful alliance between the European monarchs and the Church, but not without tension and conflicts.

Alliance between Throne and Altar

The conquistadors of the sixteenth century were another version of the alliance between throne and altar, the sword and the cross, to extend Christendom into so-called heathen territories. Mission was equated with territorial expansion and the attempt to civilize the infidels' lands. In Spain and Portugal, the relationship between the throne and the altar was very strong, and thus it was natural for them to become the first European colonizing powers and the first to send missionaries to the Far East. The main issue here is that colonialism and mission were intertwined in Catholicism at the beginning of the modern era when the pope granted royal patronage to the monarchs of Spain and Portugal. Colonization and Christianization became intimately related.

Those who sponsored and accompanied the missionaries, however, were not all equally motivated to spread the gospel. For example, Philip II of Spain emphasized "the teaching and conversion of the natives of those provinces, and the bringing them into our Holy Catholic Faith" and at the same time, he would call "for the service of God Our Lord, and for the increase to the Royal Crown of these kingdoms."[20] The missionaries were often at odds with the secular powers because of their different objectives, and they were also obliged to acknowledge this symbiotic relationship

18. Elizondo, "Evangelization Is Inculturation," 21.

19. Rodriquez, *Our Lady of Guadalupe*, 13.

20. Hutchison, *Errand to the World*, 17–18. The material in this section appeared in Mong, *Guns and Gospel*, 10–11.

between Church and state. Hostilities and also a sense of moral superiority towards cruel and unjust rulers ensued.

The case of Bartholomé de Las Casas, the sixteenth-century Spanish Dominican friar who fought against a society that approved Indian slavery, is an example of the tension between the missionaries and the colonial government. Las Casas condemned the brutality and the inhumanity of the Spanish colonists with vehemence:

> I invoke all the hierarchies and choirs of angels, all the saints of the Celestial Court, all the inhabitants of the globe to witness that I free my conscience of all that has been done . . . If [his Majesty] abandons the government of the Indies to the tyranny of the Spaniards, they will all be lost and depopulated . . . God will punish Spain and all her people with inevitable severity. So may it be.[21]

Fellow Dominican Antonio de Montesinos, who inspired Las Casas, reproached the planters of Hispaniola: "Tell me, by what right or justice do you keep these Indians in such cruel and horrible servitude? . . . You kill them with your desire to extract and acquire gold every day . . . Be certain that in such a state as this, you can no more be saved than the Moors or the Turks."[22] Resentful of the colonial government, these courageous priests felt the need to be independent from the political authorities, and from the kinds of conquest and exploitation they were forced to endorse tacitly. In general, the missionaries' refusal to cooperate with the colonizers means that from the outset, the determination to do good to the natives was more problematic than the commitment to spread the faith.

Spiritual Conquest

One of the prime motives for the conquest of Mexico was to replace the bloodthirsty idols of the Aztec with faith in Jesus Christ and love for his Blessed Mother. Christianity could not have coexisted with the Aztec religion of human sacrifices. While most of the conquistadors were greedy and violent, Carroll portrays Cortés as a devout Christian soldier who also played a major role in the spiritual conquest of Mexico. Cortés was reported to have told Montezuma, the Aztec ruler, that in times to come, "our lord and king would send men who lead holy lives, better than ourselves,

---

21. Ibid., 20.
22. Ibid.

who would explain everything [about the Christian faith], for we have come only to notify them."[23] Such spiritual humility was rare among the conquistadors.

Charles V, grandson of Queen Isabel, assumed the title of Holy Roman Emperor, temporal protector of Christendom, and officially recognized Cortés as governor and Captain-General of New Spain (Mexico) in 1522. While appreciating his great service to the nation, the King of Spain stressed Cortés's duty to convert the natives of Mexico to Christianity, and to abolish human sacrifices and idolatry there. The mendicant orders were the first to respond: Franciscan missionaries arrived in New Spain in 1524, followed by the Dominicans in 1526, and the Augustinians in 1533. These early missionaries hoped to establish an ideal Christian society in the New World, free from decadence that had corrupted the old Church in Europe.[24] In other words, they were determined to preach an "evangelical" Christianity in the New World, freed from European pagan customs that were observed in Spain.

They were influenced by writings of Joachim de Fiore, who had divided the world into three ages: the age of the Father, the age of the Son, and the age of the Spirit. The early Franciscan friars had hope that the discovery of the new world would be a place where the Spirit would flourish. It would be a new church that would retain the best of European values while avoiding all its many vices.[25]

The early Franciscans in Mexico also interpreted the conversion of Indians as a revival of the primitive church and as a divine compensation for the loss of many Catholics who had turned to Protestantism in Northern Europe as the result of the Reformation, which occurred during this period. It was a powerful justification for the establishment of the Catholic Church in Mexico. The church thus imposed a relatively standardized Catholicism throughout Latin America with "only nominal concessions to Indian beliefs and practices."[26] In spite of this policy of religious uniformity, Mexico has been successful in interweaving Spanish and native traditions in their religious practice as typified in the veneration of Our Lady of Guadalupe.

---

23. Carroll, *Our Lady of Guadalupe and the Conquest of Darkness*, 79.

24. Climenhaga, "The Huei tlamahuiçoltica," 66.

25. Elizondo, "Evangelization Is Inculturation," 20. See also Brading, *Mexican Phoenix*, 22–23.

26. Madsen, "Religious Syncretism," 369.

Twelve Franciscans who arrived in Mexico City in 1524 confounded the Aztecs with their simplicity and poverty—they walked barefoot all the way from Veracruz. When Cortez knelt before the friars as they entered the city, the Indians also fell on their knees. The austere lifestyle and self-discipline of the friars commanded respect from the Indians. The Franciscans exercised a profound influence in the conversion of the natives to Christianity. The Indians respected the self-denial attitude of the friars, which was also part of Aztec virtues. The Franciscans visited the sick, comforted the dying, and defended the natives against the cruelties of the Spanish rulers. Deeply impressed by the humility of the friars, which was such a big contrast from the arrogance and avarice of the other Spaniards, the natives called the Franciscans, *Motolinea*, or poor fellows.[27] Juan Diego was one of the earliest of the Franciscans' converts.

Juan Diego

Juan Diego was born around the year 1474 in Cauatitlán of the Texcoco Kingdom, part of the Triple Alliance with the Aztec Empire. He came from the middle class known as a *maschual* and he owned property.[28] In the year around 1524 he was baptized with his wife, María Lucia, by the Franciscan missionaries. When his wife died five years later, Juan Diego was left alone in Tulpetlac, close to Mexico City, with his elderly uncle, Juan Bernardino, another convert to Catholicism.

As a boy, Juan Diego had lived through the horrifying times of Tlacaellel's sacrifice of 80,000 people, at the arrival of Hernán Cortés and his victory over the Aztec's armies. Diego's wife, María Lucia, and his uncle, Juan Bernardino were also baptized. They were simple folks, the kind of people that God favors. The Blessed Virgin in shining clothes first appeared to Juan Diego on Saturday, December 9, 1531 when he was on his way from his village of Tulpetlac to Tlatelolco for morning mass. The Virgin expressed her desire to have a sanctuary erected so that suffering people might experience her maternal love and care. She wanted Diego to express her intention to the Bishop of Mexico, Juan Zumárraga—to build a sanctuary on the hill of Tepeyac:

---

27. Carroll, *Our Lady of Guadalupe and the Conquest of Darkness*, 83.
28. Anderson and Chávez, *Our Lady of Guadalupe*, 5.

> I want very much that they build my sacred little house here, in which I will show him, I will exalt him on making him manifest; I will give him to the people in all my personal love, in my compassionate gaze, in my help, in my salvation, because I am truly your compassionate mother, yours and of all the people who live together in this land, and of all the other people of different ancestries, my lovers, those who cry to me, those who seek me, those who trust in me.[29]

It is quite clear that the Blessed Mother wanted to bring the people closer to God through her intercession. It is also very significant that she wanted a church to be built for this purpose. For a native like Juan Diego, the establishment of a religious building like a church was more than a ceremonial occasion, it the was foundation of a society—in the past, the construction of a new temple inaugurated a new society or a new dynasty. In other words, the Virgin's command to Juan Diego was filled with symbolic meanings.[30] For example, Juan Diego Cuauhtlatoatzin's native name means "eagle that speaks." In Aztec culture, the eagle, like the sun, played a symbolic role, suggesting the dawn of a new civilization. The Virgin had requested him to be the messenger of a new epoch where the sacrifice of Christ would replace human sacrifices.[31]

It was natural for Bishop Zumárraga to be skeptical of Juan Diego's story. The bishop must haved wondered why the Blessed Virgin would appear to a newly baptized Indian. Why would the Virgin request a church to be built on Tepeyac Hill close to the peak where the ancient temple dedicated to the pagan goddess, Coatlicue, was located?[32] It was a significant request, one to which the bishop needed more time to respond. Further, the Virgin could also have appeared to the bishop himself; why did she need an intermediary? The selection of Juan Diego by the Virgin was in line with biblical tradition: "He has brought down the powerful from their thrones, and lifted up the lowly" (Luke 1: 52).

---

29. Valeriano, "Nican Mopohua," 3–4.

30. Anderson and Chávez, *Our Lady of Guadalupe*, 9–10.

31. Ibid., 23.

32. The Franciscan Fray Bernardino de Sahagún had recorded that the Tepeyac Hill once had a temple dedicated to the mother of the gods whom they called Tonantzin, which means our Mother. Sahagún was worried that the natives continued worshipping their pagan gods and goddesses under the guise of Christian veneration of the saints. In fact, Sahagún was sure that the natives had a natural tendency to relapse into idol worship even though they had been baptized Christians. Lee, "Our Lady of Guadalupe," 9.

In spite of Bishop Zumárraga's initial skepticism, the Virgin insisted that Juan Diego carry the message to the bishop again. On Sunday, December 10, Juan Diego visited the bishop after some difficulties with the guards who attempted to stop him. This time the bishop demanded proofs from him. Instead of meeting the Virgin the following day on Monday, December 11, to obtain the proof demanded by the bishop, Juan Diego went to visit his uncle, Bernardino, who fell sick. On Tuesday, December 12, Juan Diego went in search for a priest to anoint his uncle. He avoided the hill of Tepeyac out of fear and embarrassment because he did not keep his appointment with the Virgin. But the Virgin approached him with these words: "Am I not here, I who am your Mother? Are you not under my shadow and protection? Am I not the source of your joy? Are you not in the hollow of my mantle, in the crossing of my arms? Do you need something more?"[33]

Assuring him that his uncle would not die, the Virgin told Juan Diego to climb a hill and pluck flowers blooming there for her. Although the hill was a desert place where only cactus and thistles flourished, Juan Diego discovered beautiful Castilian roses with exquisite fragrance. The Virgin took the flowers from him and placed them in his *tilma*, a cloak made of fiber of the maguey cactus. The *tilma* would be a proof for the bishop that it is the Virgin's will to build a sanctuary in her honor.[34] Juan Diego was her ambassador.

When Juan Diego arrived at the bishop's residence, the roses fell to the floor, and on the *tilma* was a full portrait of the Virgin, the Mother of God, in native dress, her small hands joined in prayer with half-closed eyes.[35] This portrait still exits today in Mexico City. After 450 years, the portrait still retains its brilliant color. News spread fast and wide, many miracles were attributed to Our Lady of Guadalupe, and Pope John Paul II proclaimed her the Patroness of all the Americas in 1999 and canonized Juan Diego in Mexico City on Wednesday July 31, 2002.

Moving to Catholicism

The Aztecs were forced to abandon their religion and to accept Christianity. The Spanish were bent on destroying their idols completely and replacing

33. Valeriano, "Nican Mopohua," 10
34. Ibid., 12.
35. Ibid., 13.

them with Catholicism. The suppression of the old beliefs did not result in the immediate acceptance of the Christian faith. For nearly ten years, the Aztecs' reaction to monotheistic Christianity was negative because they hated the Spanish conquistadors whose religion was in direct conflict with their polytheistic belief. Worship of the old gods continued in Mexico City and Texcoco until 1526.[36]

Later generations of Aztecs accepted Christianity superficially without upholding its values. For example, they hid figures of the old gods behind Christian altars. Some villagers worshipped pagan deities together with Catholic saints, the Blessed Virgin, and the crucified Christ. They preferred to have more gods than just one. This joint worship of Aztec and Christian saints was the first attempt at syncretism—a fusion of Indian and Catholic forms. This practice was not new to the natives—the adding of new gods to the old had precedent in Mexican culture. They had traditionally adopted deities from various tribes that had invaded the Valley of Mexico long before the arrival of the Spaniards. The friars were very much against these kinds of syncretic practices. Thus a majority of the Indians were forced to abandon their traditional religion.[37]

It should also be noted that some Franciscan friars started their own kind of adaptation or inculturation. For example, Pedro de Gante in the Catholic liturgy used pagan songs and dances, and infused them with Christian motifs. Gante's innovation was popular and attracted hundreds of Indians to church ceremonies.[38] But these participations were rather superficial without many gospel values being imparted. The real turning point in the evangelization of the native came with the miraculous apparition of the brown face Virgin of Guadalupe in 1531. William Madsen maintains that this event brought about real conversion, the "emotional acceptance of a new faith," which he describes as "Guadalupinist Catholicism."[39]

It was natural for the Aztecs to associate Guadalupe with Tonantzin (meaning "our sacred mother" in the Nahuatl language) since both were

36. Madsen, "Religious Syncretism," 372.

37. Ibid., 376.

38. "Fray Pedro de Gante was a Franciscan lay brother who started by spending a lot of time playing with the children so that he could be reborn into the native Nahua culture. He learned their culture, their religious rites and symbols, their songs and art forms, and their language. Gante became one of them so that they could become one in Christ by evangelizing the whole psyche of the people. He was by far the greatest and most effective missionary of Mexico." Elizondo, "Evangelization Is Inculturation," 21.

39. Madsen, "Religious Syncretism," 377.

virgin mothers of gods and both appeared in the same site. In spite of the Franciscans' misgiving, Guadalupe cannot be interpreted as worshipping a goddess. In fact, the adoration of Guadalupe represented a genuine transformation of Aztec religious belief. Tonantzin was different from the Virgin Mary—her image depicts her as a monster with two streams of blood, shaped like snakes, flowing down her neck. Tonantzin was both a creator and a destroyer, very much like the deities in the Aztec pantheon. The Virgin of Guadalupe, on the other hand, is a model of beauty, love, and mercy. Not a nature goddess, Guadalupe protects her children from harms and illnesses. Her children do not have to repay her with human sacrifices; they have only to offer her flowers and candles. Among the saints that are venerated in Mexico, Our Lady of Guadalupe is the most compassionate and perfect model of Christian virtues.[40]

In sum, the Spanish conquest of the Aztec people whose cultural values were based on war and human sacrifices led to a spiritual vacuum in their lives. It produced "a strain for new religious orientations," which led to a fusion of Spanish and Indian values known as "Guadalupinist Catholicism."[41] This successful syncretism was due to the good pastoral guidance of the Franciscan friars who were able to convey the Christian faith in their native tongue, Nahuatl.

Thus, Aztec human sacrifice was transformed by the missionaries into an evangelizing symbol: Jesus of Nazareth had offered the perfect sacrifice and it was no longer necessary for other human sacrifices—this one sacrifice of Christ surpassed their previous sacrifices. Thus the crucified Christ is an important symbol in Mexican Catholicism. The Nahuas venerated the sun as a source and sustenance of life. The missionaries also transformed this devotion into *Jesus Sacramentado*—the presence of Christ in the Blessed Sacrament held by a monstrance that resembles the sun.[42]

However, the most important factor that led to this successful adaptation, or *inculturation* as we call it today, is the apparition of a dark skinned Virgin of Guadalupe to a native, Juan Diego. This miraculous appearance has helped the Indians to make Iberian Christianity their very own: Catholicism with Nahuatl characteristics. In fact, the first ten years after their defeat by the Spaniards were devastating for the natives. Life had no meaning for them, and many languished and died. Then out of the blue, in the

---

40. Ibid., 378.
41. Ibid., 389.
42. Elizondo, "Evangelization Is Inculturation," 21.

month of December 1531, the Blessed Virgin Mary appeared to an Indian at the outskirt of the city of Tenochtitlán, now present-day Mexico City, which would give hope, and change the cultural and religious landscape of Mexico.

Model of Inculturation

Our Lady of Guadalupe did not appear just for the Mexican people. In fact, her mission was extended to the rest of the world—it is first continental and then universal. She told Juan Diego that she was truly his compassionate mother and mother to all who lived on this land, and also to people of other nations who sought her help. Our Lady of Guadalupe is an inculturated figure when we look at her self-image imprinted on the *tilma* of Juan Diego—we notice that she is brown-skinned, a *mestiza* of European and native Mexican heritage.

While the Spaniards questioned the humanity of the natives, the Virgin's brown face and the declaration of her motherhood to Juan Diego affirmed the humanity of the Indians. In her mestiza face, the Indians recognized her as a person of the New World, sharing their physical traits and culture. John Paul II wrote that Juan Diego did not abandon his native identity when he became a Christian. In fact, Juan Diego discovered the profound truth about the new humanity in which we are all called to be children of God in Christ. Referring to Juan Diego's humble status, John Paul II is reminded of what Jesus has said, "I thank you, Father, Lord of heaven and earth, because you have hidden these things from the wise and the intelligent and have revealed them to infants" (Matt 11:25).[43] The Virgin's role is clearly manifested in this mystery, and in Juan Diego she has chosen one of her own.

On July 31, 2002, Pope John Paul II canonized Juan Diego Cuauhtlatoatzin in the Basilica of Our Lady of Guadalupe, Mexico City. In his apostolic exhortation, *Ecclesia in America*, John Paul II wrote:

> The appearance of Mary to the native Juan Diego on the hill of Tepeyac in 1531 had a decisive effect on evangelization. Its influence greatly overflows the boundaries of Mexico, spreading to the whole Continent. America, which historically has been, and still is, a melting-pot of peoples, has recognized in the mestiza face of

---

43. See John Paul II, *Canonization of Juan Diego Cuauhtlatoatzin*.

the Virgin of Tepeyac, "in Blessed Mary of Guadalupe, an impressive example of a perfectly inculturated evangelization."[44]

For this reason, John Paul II named Our Lady of Guadalupe Queen of All America, and on her feast day, December 12, she is declared Queen throughout the Western hemisphere.

Although the Virgin's image is addressed to an Indian, it also has a universal significance. Identifying the goodness found in indigenous culture, which lies in every civilization, she brought forth those "seeds of the Word," purifying and reaffirming them in Christ's universal salvific mission. Thus, Pope Benedict XVI held Our Lady of Guadalupe as the model of that that can unite all religious traditions together in Christ:

> Our Lady of Guadalupe is in many respects an image of the relationship between Christianity and the religions of the world: all of these streams flow together into it, are purified and renewed, but are not destroyed. It is also an image of the relationship of the truth of Jesus Christ to the truths of those religions: the truth does not destroy; it purifies and unites.[45]

This image of Guadalupe conveys more powerfully and realistically to the Indians in Mexico the truth of Christ than any profound philosophy or theology that the West can offer. Further, the Virgin spoke to Juan Diego in his own indigenous tongue, *Nahuatl*.

Mexican Catholicism

The story of Guadalupe established the foundation of Christianity in Mexico and provided a link between indigenous and European cultures. Guadalupe initiated the Christianization of Mexico and it developed the faith into "Guadalupinist Catholicism," as mentioned earlier. Our Lady of Guadalupe has become a symbol of Mexican Catholicism. Through a process of syncretism, the Aztecs adapted Catholicism according to their own cultural and religious symbols. Guadalupinist Catholicism thus spread rapidly in central Mexico and "became a focal value of Aztec culture."[46] The Virgin of Guadalupe has also become a symbol that affirms the humanness

---

44. John Paul II, *Ecclesia in America*, no. 11.
45. Anderson and Chávez, *Our Lady of Guadalupe*, 40.
46. Madsen, "Religious Syncretism," 378.

of the indigenous people and forges a new cultural identity for Mexico by uniting both Spanish and native elements.

Devotion to Our Lady of Guadalupe spread far and wide; copies of her imprint on the *tilma* of Juan Diego can be found throughout the world. Virgilio P. Elizondo argues that the story of Our Lady of Guadalupe actually begins in 1492 when Europeans encountered the Amerindian civilization. The two cultures could not be more different—they were fascinated by and feared each other at the same time. Due to a number of factors described earlier, especially technological superiority in warfare and the spread of diseases, the Aztec civilization was almost completely wiped out by the Spaniard forces. But the native culture survived in some ways, in Mexican Christianity, due to the apparition on the Tepeyac Hill in 1531, just ten years after the conquest of Mexico. When the natives were suffering so much, the dark Virgin Mary appeared to Juan Diego to show her love and compassion for his people.[47] The apparition was Mary's response to the cries of the poor.

Elizondo maintains that the story of the apparition is a creative narrative of compassion remembered by the victims and survivors of the Spanish brutal conquest—these people were the "firstborn of the new creation." European historians wrote about the conquest and destruction, whereas Nahua historians gave us a creation story—the *Nican Mopohua*.[48] With a mixture of Nahuatl and Iberian symbols and styles, this simple poem which is audio, together with the *tilma* which is visual, communicate the compassionate love of God through the Blessed Virgin Mary.

Devotion to Our Lady of Guadalupe has kept the gospel alive by transmitting the message of Christ through songs, dances, and personal testimonies. Loved by the natives, the metizos and criollos, today Guadalupe is embraced by the poor, marginalized, and downtrodden. Elizondo points out that the Guadalupe story is "strikingly simple," like the gospel narratives: "It is the Nahuatl proclamation of the Resurrection: 'They tried to kill us, but God has raised us to life. They tried to destroy the ways of life of our ancestors, but God has protected us and redeemed us.'"[49]

For Mexican immigrants in the Southwest of the United States, despised by the Anglophones in a Protestant nation, Guadalupe gives a sense of pride and dignity. Our Lady of Guadalupe has helped to keep the Mexican

---

47. Poole and Elizondo, "Guadalupe, Nuestra Señora de."
48. Ibid.
49. Ibid.

culture alive in a foreign land—it gives Mexicans living in the United States a sense of cohesion and belonging, especially among the immigrant farm workers. Regarded as a protector and liberator of the poor and marginalized, the Virgin of Guadalupe is also seen as the "mother of a new humanity," manifesting the femininity of God. She is not just a story about the past, but a living presence when the faithful continues to re-create and transmit her message of love and peace. She is a symbol of reconciliation among races both in the Americas and elsewhere such as South Africa. Elizondo makes it clear to us that Our Lady of Guadalupe is not part of Catholic dogma. It is popular piety, a devotion that arises from the heart, the saving truth that is found in the faith of the people, *sensus fidelium*.[50] As a popular piety, devotion to Our Lady of Guadalupe transmits more powerfully and tangibly the mystery of God's presence among the poor and dispossessed.

Conflicting Claims

The Guadalupe story is a typical account of the Virgin Mary's apparitions such as those that occurred in Lourdes, Fatima, and Medjugorje, in that she appeared to poor and humble people, and the bishop of that place was skeptical in the beginning, but was won over by miracles. However, the apparition in Guadalupe is different in that the Virgin's message is not apocalyptic; it does not speak of the end times, but is comforting and protective news for the present. There were many references to a chapel at Guadalupe between 1556 and 1648, but there was no mention of the apparition. It has been established that the shrine was built between 1555 and 1556, not in 1531.[51] Thus from the beginning, this apparition of Mary has been shrouded in controversies with conflicting accounts, claims, and interpretations.

Some historians viewed the Christianization of Mexico as "conversion by sword," a by-product of colonization, and the Guadalupe story is a strategic devotion calculated to pacify the native Indians with a concocted Christian-Aztec story. It can also be interpreted as a subversive Christian piety adopted by the Indians to preserve some elements of their Aztec religious heritage. As such the Catholicity of Guadalupan devotees is very much contested.

Perhaps the symbol of Christian victory in the New World is the construction of churches on the sites of former Aztec temples. While early

50. Ibid.
51. Ibid.

missionaries were eager to display the truth of Christianity over pagan religions, they were also careful to cultivate a sense of continuity with the Nahuas' religious sensibility, such as their sense of sacred places. In practice, it was a more complicated and ambiguous affair because the reality is that "much less of the pre-Hispanic religion was destroyed and much more was recycled, because it was relatively easily Christianized (or was it that Christianity was relatively easily indigenized and mestizized?)."[52]

Miguel Sánchez, a Mexican priest, in his book *Imagen de la Virgen María, Madre de Dios de Guadalupe* (1648), attempted to give an explanation for the origin of the shrine by asserting that the apparition is a divine endorsement of the special status of the *criollos*, Mexicans of European descent, and the city of Mexico. This story came as a surprise to the natives of Mexico. It was also claimed that the story of the apparition was "forgotten" for over 150 years.[53]

Luis Laso de la Vega, the vicar of the shrine at Guadalupe, published a book in Nahuatl, *Huei tlamahuiçoltica*, intended for the indigenous population. In Vega's text, he included an account of the apparition known as *Nican mopohua*—miracle stories (*Nican motecpana*) and devotional materials (*Nican tlantica*). This book had little influence on the natives. In fact, before the eighteenth century, devotion to Our Lady of Guadalupe was confined to the *criollo* population in Mexico. In 1736, an epidemic struck Mexico City and both the government and the church made an oath in accepting Guadalupe as the patroness of the city with its feast day on December 12. This patronage spread quickly to the rest of Mexico and the Spanish empire.[54]

There is no evidence that the apparition at Guadalupe brought millions of natives to Christianity, according to Poole and Elizondo. It was only during the last half of the eighteenth century that devotion to Our Lady of Guadalupe spread among the indigenous population in Mexico as part of the campaign of the church.[55] Popular piety is often promoted by ecclesiastical authorities and is not a spontaneous development, as is commonly held.

In the revolution of 1810, Miguel de Hidalgo y Costilla used Guadalupe as a symbol of Mexican nationality, a force that unites disparate classes

52. Climenhaga, "The Huei tlamahuiçoltica," 68.
53. Poole and Elizondo, "Guadalupe, Nuestra Señora de."
54. Ibid.
55. Ibid.

and various ethnic groups in society. Guadalupe has also been interpreted as a kind of "spiritual orphanhood," in which we see a comforting mother giving hope to a native population that has been crushed by Spanish colonization. In this spiritual image, the Church and the Spanish crown were forced to recognize the humanity and dignity of the indigenous population. Guadalupe can also be seen as an instrument of evangelization, which united the "indigenous past to the Spanish present" and thus established the modern Mexican society.[56]

Hence, some preachers had maintained that the foundation of Mexico could be dated from the apparition of the Virgin at Tepeyac in 1531 when she liberated the natives from the old religion and Spanish tyranny. The Virgin is considered the founder of the new mestizo community when she reconciled the Spaniards and Indians, united them in the faith as one nation. Manual Ignacio Altamirano, a journalist, maintained that "for the Mexicans, in the last extreme, in the most desperate cases, the cult of the Mexican Virgin is the only bond which unites them."[57]

The devotion to Guadalupe is now a peaceful cult: Catholics venerated the Virgin as part of popular piety in Catholicism; liberals honored the image as the flag of 1810 and the Indians still adored her as their only goddess. Altamirano, thus, concluded that "the day in which the Virgin of Tepeyac is not adored in this land it is certain that there shall have disappeared, not only Mexican nationality, but also the very memory of the dwellers of Mexico today."[58]

In terms of inculturation, Guadalupe is an example of presenting Christian teaching in native forms. Whatever interpretations theologians and social scientists may give to the Guadalupe phenomenon, the question of historical truth and validity of the apparition seldom emerge. What is crucial is the impact and significance of the apparition on the lives of the faithful, the evolution of the cult, and the response of the ecclesiastical authorities. Regarding these issues, popular piety in the Philippines presents an interesting case study, which will be the subject of the next chapter.

---

56. Ibid. As a symbol of national unity, the Mexican revolution was fought literally under the banner of Our Lady of Guadalupe and in her defense. See Lafaye, *Quetzalcóatl and Guadalupe*.

57. Brading, *Mexican Phoenix*, 9.

58. Ibid., 257.

Chapter 3

Pinoy Piety

Popular piety in the Philippines is a fascinating subject to explore. Like the countries in Latin America, this Asian nation is predominantly Roman Catholic with four centuries of Christian presence. The result of syncretism, a blending of elements from its indigenous culture and traditional faith, popular piety retains its vitality as folk Catholicism with its power to shape the lives of individuals, of families as well as of the community at large. Catholics in the Philippines find strength and consolation in their popular religion. In the midst of sufferings and oppression, they resort to popular cultural expressions of their faith.

Popular piety has also its downside, as we have noted earlier—it can be a kind of escapism, a refusal to face the harsh realities of life, an immature faith that leads to passivity, fatalism, and superstition. Popular religion has also been manipulated by political leaders to pacify the people and to strengthen the leaders' hold on the masses by encouraging pious practices, beliefs that stress the value of suffering as a means to eternal happiness, thus curtailing their efforts to transform society for the better. Another negative aspect of popular religion is the presence of superstitious beliefs and practices such as predicting the future, dream interpretation, communication with the spirits, and wearing good luck charms and amulets.

This chapter attempts a short survey of popular piety in the Philippines, with a critical focus on the veneration of Santo Niño of Cebu, and of the suffering Christ, and devotion to Our Lady of Perpetual Help. These three forms of piety are the most prominent in Filipino folk Catholicism. Filipinos have an ardent devotion to the Blessed Virgin Mary, due in part to the Hispanic roots of Filipino Catholicism and the society's esteem and respect for women, especially mothers. This chapter also attempts to explain why Christianity, Catholicism in particular, could flourish on Filipino soil in spite of the people's resentment of Spanish colonization. Before the arrival of the Spaniards, the pre-Christian belief of Filipinos was cosmic in origin.

Cosmic and Metacosmic Religions

Sri Lankan Jesuit Aloysius Pieris says Asiatic religions consist of two complementary elements: a cosmic feature that constitutes its foundation, and a metacosmic soteriology that constitutes its structure.[1] Cosmic religion is sometimes negatively referred to as animism by Western writers, but Pieris argues that it presents a basic human attitude towards the mysteries of life relating to forces such as earth, water, wind, and fire. Fire and water feature also in the Catholic celebration of the Paschal Mystery.

Furthermore, in Asia, cosmic religion does not appear in its primordial form but is integrated into one of the three metacosmic soteriologies—Hinduism, Buddhism, and Taoism. In other words, these three religions are fused with the cosmic religions in a given culture. Unlike African cosmic religions, they are not regarded as salvific, and this is of great significance for Asian theology. For example, belief in *devas* is accommodated in Buddhism but they (*devas*) are not given any soteriological power over people. The Buddha placed Nirvana above everything else. In Asian forms of Buddhism, the cosmic forces of the ancient past are subordinated to the metacosmic goal of the Buddhist religion.[2] Pieris also says that Buddhists do not confuse one with the other.

We see the same thing regarding cosmic and metacosmic religion occurring in Indonesia, where Islam is the official religion, and in the Philippines, where 80 percent of the people profess Catholicism. Within these two world religions, the native folk traditions or animistic beliefs are somewhat tolerated but subordinated. Pieris points out that the ancient cosmic religions in Indonesia and in the Philippines were "undomesticated" by other metacosmic religions such as Hinduism and Buddhism and, thus, Islam and Catholicism respectively were able to establish a firm foundation there. However, in Sri Lanka, India, and Myanmar and other South

---

1. Some material in this chapter appeared in Mong, *Accommodation and Acceptance*, 83–86.
2. Ibid.

Asian countries, neither Islam nor Christianity can penetrate these cultures because gnostic soteriologies (e.g., Hinduism and Buddhism) had already accommodated themselves with the local cosmic forces.[3] This explains why Christianity, he believes, has failed to take root in most parts of Asia in spite of centuries of missionary toil. Given this understanding of cosmic and metacosmic religions, it is unlikely that Sri Lanka, Thailand, or Myanmar will ever be Christian nations just as it is unlikely that the Philippines will become a Buddhist country.

Helicopter Theory

The expansion of Buddhism, Christianity, and Islam shows that the cosmic religions have served as "helicopter pads" on which these metacosmic religions have landed, as it were. Thus, if one helicopter has already landed, there will be no space for another. In other words, if a metacosmic religion has taken root in a culture supported by its cosmic religion, it will not be easy for another to grow there. Pieris calls this observation based on sociological research is called "Helicopter Theory of Religious Expansion."[4] As mentioned earlier, Christianity had spread through the Philippines but at the same time, it had failed to take hold in India, Sri Lanka, and other societies that were already Hindu, Buddhist, or Muslim. These religions had arrived early, sunk their roots in the cultures, and fused with the local cosmic religions. It is on a "first come, first served" basis, as it were.

Pieris has observed that in places where the cosmic religiosity still prevails, for example in parts of Laos, Cambodia, the tribal regions of India, and South Korea where Buddhism is more Confucian (more cosmic in other words) in its outlook, there is a chance that Christianity may succeed in establishing itself. Further, in certain parts of Indonesia like North Sumatra, Ambonia, and Moluccas, conversion to Christianity is easier because the cosmic religiosity there has a stronger influence over the people than Islam. Other than these places, Christianity has little chance of spreading to the rest of Asia. Of course, Pieris does not rule out that things may change due to political or military interventions or through mass migration, but the fact that Asia still remains non-Christian after so many centuries of evangelization gives us food for thought and reflection.[5] Pieris is convinced

3. Pieris, *An Asian Theology of Liberation*, 72.
4. Pieris, *The Genesis of an Asian Theology of Liberation*, 121.
5. Pieris, *Fire and Water*, 67.

that God is revealing to us through this historical-social reality that there is another approach to proclaiming the gospel and another way of being Christian.

Pope John Paul II in his encyclical *Redemptoris Missio* wrote: "The growth in the number of new churches in recent times should not deceive us. Within the territories entrusted to these churches—particularly in Asia, but also in Africa, Latin America and Oceania—there remain vast regions still to be evangelized."[6] John Paul II singles out Asia as a vast field for evangelization—"Open the doors to Christ." But Pieris thinks there is no room for Christ as known and theologically presented in the West because the other great religions have already firmly established themselves and integrated with Asian cultures, absorbing 90 percent of its population. Perhaps the only space left is for Christ to become one of the cosmic powers, which means Jesus will be just one more deity among the pantheon of cosmic forces.[7] As we shall see, folk Catholicism in the Philippines seems to tolerate polytheism.

Pre-Christian Belief System

Animists, Filipino natives in pre-Hispanic times, believed that spirits inhabited space and time, and needed to be venerated or placated. They also believed in one Supreme Being, the all-powerful creator whom they called *Bathalang Maykapal*. The word *Bathala* seems to have originated from Sanskrit, *Bhattara*, or the highest of the gods. No one knew where *Bathala* came from, he simply appeared. Humanlike, he was strong and powerful and demanded obedience from people. He loved those who kept his commands and paid him homage. Filipinos depended on *Bathala* to do everything for them—they thus adopted this casual mentality, *Bahala na* ("let whatever happen"), an attitude that is rather passive, or carefree, or reckless.[8] This attitude still holds true today to some extent.

Since Filipinos' primitive religious belief consisted of spirits, the *Bathala* was everywhere and thus there was no need for particular places for sacrifice and worship, which included praise and adoration. For the locals, this act of worship or sacrifice was for material benefits such as avoiding evil, recovery from illness, a safe trip, a good harvest, a happy marriage,

---

6. John Paul II, *Redemptoris Missio*, no. 37.
7. Pieris, *Fire and Water*, 67.
8. "Bathala, the Tagalog God."

or successful childbirth. These religious beliefs were often transmitted through songs and music, and passed down from generation to generation.[9]

Successful Adaptation

Like the Christian God, Bathala is compassionate but demands justice when people break his commandments. He strikes sinners with thunder and lightning and also rules over lesser gods who take care of the needs of devout people. With the arrival of Spanish missionaries in the Philippines in the sixteenth century, *Bathala* naturally came to be associated with the Christian God and is referred to as *Panginoon* in Tagalog or *Diyos* (adapted from Spanish, *Dios*).[10] In fact, the Spanish missionaries adopted this word, *Bathala*, in their preaching. One of them wrote:

> As for their sacrifices, each one of the natives, so far as I have seen, has in his house many idols, to whom they pray. They call God, Batala (Bathala), and the chief idol which they have is thus named; but others call him Diobata (Diwata)—at least among the Pintados [term used by Spanish to describe indigenous people with tattooed bodies in Cebu, Bohol, Samar and Leyte] they give him this name. The natives of this island (Luzon) usually call him Batala, and even consider him God of all creation. Accordingly, after the religious came to this land and commenced to preach the faith of Jesus Christ, and to baptize, the natives have not known how to give any other name in their language to God our Lord, except that of Batala.[11]

A well-documented study by W. H. Scott reveals a striking resemblance between the Tagal people's ancient religious belief and folk Catholicism. The Tagal believed in a supreme God creator of the world (*Bathala*) who could be petitioned through lesser deities (*anito*) or ancestor worship. This system is quite similar to Catholicism with its veneration of saints, angels and archangels, prayers for dead, the celebration of All Souls' and All Saints' Days. Thus folk Catholicism, expressed in a variety of popular pieties, can be seen as an extension of the indigenous religious tradition in the Philippines. This popular religion is colorful and vibrant and it fulfills the need of the people to experience a glimpse of the supernatural with images, rituals,

---

9. Rios, "A continuing theology from the margins," 119.
10. "Bathala, the Tagalog God."
11. "TAGALOGS Origin Myths."

music, and dance, adapted from local culture. A brief survey of popular religion in the Philippines will help us to appreciate its varieties of form and expression.

A General Survey

Popular pieties abound in the Philippines, a country that prides itself as the only Christian country in South Asia. Catholicism having been introduced in the country during its colonization by Spain more than four centuries ago, these practices, though colored with local customs and traditions, are steeped in Spanish influence. A number of them have evolved into festivals that attract local and foreign tourists alike. Worthy of note is the *Sinulog Festival,* which is connected with devotion to the Holy Child by the natives of Cebu City, the prime city in the Visayan group of islands which is the repository of Magellan's cross. Held on the third week of January, the highlight of the festival is a carnival-like parade that features participants in colorful native regalia, and depicts local customs, livelihood, and industries.[12]

The island province of Marinduque in the Visayas is likewise noted for the Moriones Festival during Holy Week. This local custom features participants who wear the costumes and outsized masks of the Roman soldiers who participated in the capture and crucifixion of the Christ. They go around the parish searching for their missing colleague, the one-eyed Longinus. Penitential practice during Holy Week is at its most extreme, however, in San Fernando, Pampanga, in the island of Luzon, where penitents flagellate themselves with barbed whips and end up being actually nailed on crosses. The practice has become so gory it has earned the opprobrium of the local church hierarchy.

Devotion to the Black Nazarene is, on the other hand, associated with the Quiapo Church in the City of Manila. The nine-day Novena in the first week of January is capped by a procession that, of late, has lasted more than twenty-four hours and been participated in by (ever increasing) millions. The float bearing the image is borne through the streets of the city on the shoulders of chosen devotees who go about the task barefoot as a sign of penance and unity with the sufferings of their patron. The statue of the Black Nazarene is believed to be miraculous and exceedingly generous

---

12. I am very grateful to Hon. Vivencio Gregorio Atutubo III, district judge, Pili, Philippines, for providing me with firsthand knowledge on popular pieties discussed in this section.

with petitions from the faithful. Color-coded candles, corresponding to petitions regarding the health, career, relationships, and general good fortune of petitioners and/or their loved ones, are sold year-round in the vicinity of the church. Petitioners approaching the church altar on their knees are, to this day, a common sight after Masses at the Quiapo Church on Fridays—the day of the week consecrated to the patron.

Marian in nature, the Feast of Our Lady of Penafrancia is the pride of the Bicol Region, on the southern part of Luzon. Held in Naga City starting Friday of the second week of September, this nine-day feast attracts local and foreign Marian devotees, seeking the intercession of the Mother of Christ for their intentions. The festivity starts with the *traslacion* or procession transferring the statue of the virgin mother from the Penafrancia Basilica Menore to the Naga City Cathedral. While masses at the Cathedral are sponsored by various religious and civic organizations, the city abounds with a wide array of parades, exhibits, pageants, and contests. The feast culminates with a fluvial procession that, to the shouts of *Viva La Virgen,* sees the statue of the Holy Virgin home to its basilica.

The municipality of Buhi in the province of Camarines Sur is noted for its wide array of popular pieties. At Christmas time, groups of lads, lasses, and children go around the town as *Pastores* and *Pastoras,* singing olden *castilian* carols while dancing to the accompanying music from a four-man band. Entirely divorced from the image of shepherds at the Nativity, the girls and lasses are clad in white satin dresses and flowered hats, their steps timed to the clacking of their castanets. The boys and lads wear what look like white Navy gala uniforms and wield garlanded bows that they swing and twist to the beat of the music. With approval and appreciation coming in the form of *bitor* or coins thrown by spectators, participants usually have histories of ailment during their infancy and participate to fulfill a promise their parents made for their recovery.

Holy Week and Easter are observed with an even greater variety of popular pieties. As in other parts of the country, there is a *pabasa* or *pasyon* in households—a chanting of the account of Christ's passion.[13] Either chanters are hired for this tradition or family members take turns at chanting the narrative in the local vernacular. Other families would stage the *senakulo,* also a chanted dialogue between Mary and Jesus on the eve of the

---

13. The *Pasyon* is a book written in seven Filipino languages that narrates the history of salvation history from the moment of creation to the second coming of Christ. It is a prayerful meditation on the passion of Christ consisting of 3,150 rhymed stanzas of five lines each. Chupungco, *Liturgical Inculturation,* 104.

latter's passion. Reducing spectators to tears in years gone by, the highlight of the *senakulo* is the Blessed Mother's lament over her son's destiny and leave-taking.

More affluent families would also sponsor the *Tanggal,* a staging of the Passion by a band of actors who are, themselves, fulfilling pledges of their own. Before the dramatization of the Passion, highlights from the Old and New Testaments are featured in tableaus while passages from the Bible are chanted by a chorus. The presentation of the Passion featured a cast who also sang their lines as they depicted events from Christ's entry to Jerusalem up to the Resurrection. After the passion came the *Moro-moro,* a staging of St. Helena's search for the true cross, complete with colorful costumes, sung verses, and sword fights between Christians and infidels, performed to a lively tune provided by a band.

Affluent families also maintained elaborate floats or *caros* depicting scenes from the Passion—among them the Last Supper, St. Peter, the agony in the garden, Christ's indictment, the scourging at the pillar, crowning with thorns, crucifixion, the pieta or *angustia,* the *Santo Intierro,* the *tres Marias,* and the Mater Dolorosa. These floats were featured during the Holy Wednesday and Good Friday evening processions, all lit up with colorful lanterns and accompanied by a band of musicians. Of note are the *Sayos* or penitents among the womenfolk who, clad in black veils, long black robes, and only black socks for footwear, join these processions while carrying poles bearing tokens from the Passion. Much later, on the night of Good Friday, another procession called the *Soledad* is held from the opposite direction of the earlier processions. More sedate and featuring only the float of the *Mater Dolorosa,* this procession is participated in by the town's Marian devotees.

Dawn of Easter Sunday is for the *salubong*—a meeting between the Blessed Mother and the risen Christ. So ubiquitous is this ritual that most churchyards all over the Philippines have a tower or *castillo* solely devoted for this one event in the liturgical year. Mostly through popular contests in aid of the parish fundraising drive, children are chosen to act as the angels in attendance during this mother-son encounter. Lowered from a great height, the winner makes his/her contrived celestial descent from an inverted pyramid that opens into the shape of a star; and more importantly, the winner is reserved the privilege of divesting Mary's statue of the mourning veil while singing verses in Latin.

Consecrated to the Virgin Mary, the month of May is a time for popular pieties of the Marian kind. Among children, this is the season of the *Flores de Mayo* where, singing hymns of praise, they shower the statue of the Blessed Mother with flower petals. Aside from that held at the parish church, this ritual is likewise performed at affluent households that host banquets afterwards. Another May observance is the *Santacruzan,* a variant of the homage to St. Helena's search for the true cross. This local pageantry of sorts is participated in by the town's young men, escorting young maidens all dressed up as titled queens, foremost among whom is the *Reina Elena,* with the boy Constantine in tow.

Spanish in origin, these practices have been imbued with local customs, traditions, and beliefs that have transformed them into their present enculturated form. Some, like the *Sinulog Festival,* the Feast of Our Lady of Penafrancia, the *Pastores* and *Pastoras, Angelitos* and *Angelitas,* the *Flores de Mayo,* and the *Santa Cruzan* cater to the people's love of song, dance, pageantry, revelry, and *fiestas*. More than ways of currying church indulgences, others such as sponsorship of the *tanggal* and *Moro-moro* or the maintenance of *caros* for the Holy Week processions, are matters of family honor and distinction. Still others, like the devotion to the Black Nazarene, the penitential practices of the *Sayos,* and the San Fernando flagellants and sundry roles performed from pledges have been attributed to superstition and fanaticism. Like cathedral stained glass windows, however, these popular pieties offer the faithful extra-liturgical prisms through which the many aspects of their faith can be viewed and actively experienced.

Successful adaptation of Christianity to indigenous culture in the Philippines, however, did not lead to a happy outcome so far. It is really tragic that in spite of the spread of Christianity that preaches love, peace, and justice, Filipinos were not spared from the cruelty and exploitation of the Spanish conquistadors. In fact, the locals had to endure systematic degradation of their native culture through physical destruction of towns and villages, imposition of heavy taxes, and confiscation of properties. In addition, there was also enslavement of both the lower class (timawas) and even the nobility (maharlikas).[14]

Even today, when Spanish domination has long since been replaced by elected government, rampant corruption from top to bottom in both public and private sectors keeps the people in poverty. To survive, millions of Filipinos have to leave to foreign countries to seek all kinds of employment,

---

14. Rios, "A continuing theology from the margins," 119.

including domestic help, health care, information technology, etc. The remittances from these overseas workers have helped families at home, but there are also serious consequences such as absentee parents, broken families, and brain drain. Filipinos also have to endure natural calamities such as typhoons, floods, and earthquakes, situations worsened by the government's failure to provide basic infrastructures.

The sufferings that Filipinos endured through the centuries have made them not only more resilient in the face of tragedies and setbacks, but have also made them very persistent and faithful in their religious belief, which is woven in the fabric of their culture. One of the most popular devotions in Filipino folk Catholicism is the veneration of the image of Santo Niño or Infant Jesus. "Take away the image [Santo Niño] and the Philippines loses the diadem of her Christianity."[15]

Santo Niño de Cebu

Devotion to Santo Niño is perhaps the start of the foundation of the Catholic faith in the Philippines. The image of the Holy Infant was a gift given to Juana, the local queen, by Magellan at her baptism in 1521. This led to many conversions from paganism to Catholicism. Such peaceful transition from one belief to another is characterized as "the irreversible mystical process of proto-conversion and proto-evangelization."[16] In this case, it involved the miraculous power of the Child Jesus substituting the magical power of *anito*, the local deity. This is a classic example of acculturation of Christianity into folk culture—a gradual shift from pagan to Christian belief system. This kind of folk Catholicism still retains vestiges of pagan beliefs.

When formal evangelization took place with the Legazpi expedition in 1565, the natives embraced the Christian faith without much difficulties—the indigenous belief was absorbed into the structure of Roman Catholicism. Local practices such as the *sinulug* or "ritual dance" blended smoothly with Catholic symbolism and practices, thus contributing to the development of Filipino Christian culture. After forty-four years, from 1521 (arrival of Magellan) to 1565 (Legazpi expedition), the Cebuanos claimed Santo Niño as their very own: "This cognitive paradigm shift is a synchronism which started the largely successful and spontaneous overthrow of pagan

15. Dingayan, "Popular Religion and Evangelization," 356.
16. Sala-Boza, "Towards Filipino Christian Culture," 281.

religion and its replacement, at the same place and period in time by what is seen here as Christian mysticism."[17]

In other words, there was already a well-defined system of mystical beliefs and practices when Magellan arrived in Cebu, on the shores of the Philippines. Evangelization by Spanish friars resulted in the indigenous culture being superimposed by a more established religious structure, Iberian Catholicism, in which the veneration of the Infant Jesus played an important role.

In this popular piety, Catholic practices include the following: veneration of the original image of Santo Niño at the Basilica, novenas, prayers, petitioning, thanksgiving, lighting of candles, and changing the image's clothes before the fiesta. Local folk practices include fulfilling vows, offering of gifts, wiping of the image with handkerchief, and the traditional *sinulug* ritual dance. There are also civil practices such as the *sinulug* parades and other fiesta entertainment.

Catholic pious practices and devotions took root in Filipino soil due to the fact that the Spanish friars' own brand of folk Catholicism had some similarities with the religious practices of the natives, such as belief in a supreme being presiding over the universe spirits, belief in the existence of angels, and veneration of saints. Of course, this is a generalization. Some of the early missionaries from Spain were scholars and theologians. Later, however, there were also many friars from the convents in Spain who were simple peasants without higher education who brought with them religious practices and ways of relating to God to which the natives' ways of worship could be adapted.[18]

Unlike Protestantism, folk Catholicism accommodates and tolerates some form of polytheism. Roman Catholicism remains strong in the Philippines in spite of fierce proselytization by American evangelicals since the early twentieth century and the Filipinos' fondness of American culture in contrast to their resentment against the Spanish friars in the past.

The Cult of Santo Niño is essentially a syncretism of Catholic indigenous practices, and civil activities. This devotion is immensely popular even during the twentieth and twenty-first centuries, partly because it serves as a tourist attraction and also partly because of the flexibility in which the Catholic Church incorporates images taken from the local culture.

17. Ibid., 284.
18. Macdonald, "Folk Catholicism and Pre-Spanish Religions in the Philippines," 87–88.

Critical Reflection

A pastor of the United Church of Christ in the Philippines, Luna Dingayan, believes the image Santo Niño was brought by the Spanish colonizers to pacify the natives. In Spain, devotion to Santo Niño can be understood in relation to their 800 years of suffering and oppression under the Moors as a result of which Spanish Christianity is characterized by a profound sense of tragedy and death. Ironically or perhaps naturally, it seems that the Spaniards treated the Filipinos the way they had been treated by the Moors.

Popular piety such as devotion to Santo Niño could work in both directions: firstly, it could be a good expression of repentance and renewal after being liberated from bondage; secondly, such religious practice could also be encouraged so that people remain passive and simply accept the unjust situation. For example, during the time of the dictatorship under President Marcos, propagation of this kind of popular piety was used to enhance the interests of his family and cronies.[19] However, as we shall see, the image of Santo Niño was co-opted into Filipino nationalism as a symbol of protest against Spanish domination.

Poverty is a complex problem that cannot be alleviated by simply offering prayers to Santo Niño. Such devotion could be alienating, promoting "a culture of passivity, fatalism and superstition."[20] In other words, adherence to the image of the Infant Jesus could consciously or unconsciously perpetuate the situation of poverty and injustice. It could be seen as opium for the people. However, images can also be liberating if they symbolize the realities of people's living conditions, expectations, and hopes. In fact, in the history of the Philippines, Santo Niño had been co-opted as a symbol of protest against Spanish rule.

Anti-Colonial Icon

At the end of the nineteenth century, Santo Niño was utilized by some political activists in Cebu as an anti-colonial symbol. This icon, crafted in Spain, was used as a symbol of nationalism against Spanish domination: "The national 'awakening' inscribed in anti-colonial revolution frames this as a specifically subversive loyalty in which, through the Santo Niño, Cebuano revolutionaries imagined a future autonomous from the designs of

---

19. Dingayan, "Popular Religion and Evangelization," 357.
20. Ibid., 358.

the Spanish empire."[21] In Santo Niño, Cebuanos found a figure that can foster hope and expectation of being freed from oppression, and can also help to facilitate social and political change in the city. The locals reappropriate this Western icon in a "Filipinized" form signified by dressing the figure in local attire and thus making it an emblem of anti-colonial revolution.[22]

On April 3, 1898, a group of professionals and gentry clashed with Spanish soldiers at Veleriano Weyler Street (later renamed Tres de Abril Street) in Cebu. Inspired by anti-Spanish sentiments in Manila, the revolutionaries led by Pantaleon Villegas (Leon Kilat), in collaboration with a secret society known as Katipunan, decided to overthrow the Spanish armed forces in Cebu. They were able to force the colonial troops into the Spanish headquarters, Fort San Pedro. As the Spanish soldiers withdrew, crying, "Viva España!," the revolutionaries shouted triumphantly: "Mabuhi ang Katipunan! Mabuhi ang Santo Niño! " (Long live the Katipunan! Long live the Santo Niño!)[23]

Unfortunately, the success of this event, now known as the *Tres de Abril* uprising, was short-lived. Spanish warships arrived, reprisal was quick and violent, and many Cebuanos were killed, including the leader Leon Kilat. The Spanish regained control of the city. Nevertheless, the brief victory of the Tres de Abril uprising was of great significance compared to the dismal failure of other anti-Spanish campaigns in Manila. As far as the Cebuanos were concerned, the victory was brought about by the Santo Niño icon, which means the uprising had divine support, even if it was for a short duration. It also represents the victory of folk Catholicism, assisted by Santo Niño in no small measure, against its official proponent. A revolution icon, Santo Niño symbolizes "syncretistic or 'folk' modes of Catholic faith."[24] Furthermore, there is also a biblical understanding of this *Tres de Abril* uprising. It represents the child Jesus wandering away from his parents during the Festival of the Passover. Jesus was later found in the temple talking to the Pharisees. The independence of the twelve-year-old child, Jesus, was not lost to Cebuanos, seeking independence from the Mother country.

21. Bautista, "The Rebellion and the Icon," 294.
22. Ibid., 295.
23. Ibid., 296.
24. Ibid., 297.

The Suffering Christ

Filipino popular piety is also characterized by the devotion to the suffering Christ who becomes their liberator and savior. This is different from the image of Christ the liberator as portrayed in Latin American liberation theology, who is a political or social reformer. In the context of the Philippines, Christ the liberator "is that of the pasyon, the suffering Christ who died and rose again without necessarily fighting back his enemies."[25] Matthew Rios writes: "Their sympathy with the suffering Jesus led the masses to recognize the sinfulness of their *loob* (inner self) and led them to believe in the replacement of their individual and communal darkness and misery with an era of liberation and freedom."[26] Preoccupation with the suffering Christ also leads to the development of local penitential practices such as flagellation and moving on their knees to the church. The image of Christ is associated with the language of sacrifice, which is part of Filipino culture. In traditional religious practice, the sacrificial killing of pigs and chickens was common.

Filipinos value harmonious relationship above all. This implies that they are tolerant, inclusive, and adaptable, rather than rigid adherents of rules and structures. Rios puts it this way: "They [Filipinos] are not so disposed to the rational analysis of disjunctive either/or thinking and will usually shrink from distinctions and objectifications."[27] Filipinos are concerned with maintaining harmony in the families, in the community and society at large. This emphasis on harmony, tolerance, and unity is clearly manifested in their popular piety, especially during the processions for the *Hesus Nazareno* (Jesus the Nazarene). Here we witness people from all walks of life, including the clergy and petty pickpockets, students and teachers, marching together with their attention fixed on the sufferings of Christ with whom all can relate. The devotion to the *Hesus Nazareno* is a reflection of the people's own sufferings and their need for healing and liberation.

Known also as the Black Nazarene, the image of *Hesus Nazareno* is found in Quiapo Church, downtown Manila. It was the work of an unknown Mexican artist who was brought to the Philippines in the seventeenth century. The image, dressed in purple and wearing a crown of thorns, kneeling

---

25. Rios, "A continuing theology from the margins," 125.
26. Ibid.
27. Ibid.

on one leg and carrying a cross on its shoulder, is a powerful symbol that evokes strong emotions and devotions.

On the feast day of the Black Nazarene, January 9, the image is paraded through the streets of Manila, amid throngs of fervent devotees who crowd around in order to touch the figure. Wearing white t-shirts, with jeans rolled up, barefooted, towels around their neck, the men from the squatter areas make vows that they will fulfill in the following years in honor of the Black Nazarene. This image of the Christ is "a witness to the incarnation of God, to the reality of God's presence and to participation in the very life of God."[28]

Filipinos tend to feel extremely vulnerable to the evils of the world, and thus a figure like the suffering Christ, kneeling on one knee, can offset this cosmic sense of fear and weakness. This image, *Hesus Nazareno*, gives people confidence, a sense of invincibility, when they perform the ritual faithfully. It also brings together people from all walks of life and narrows the gap between God and the human person because the suffering Christ is portrayed as black and down to earth.

Filipino Flagellation

Filipino piety emphasizes vision, image, and ritual rather than theological or philosophical speculations. In their piety, Filipinos want to experience the effect of the supernatural in their lives and thus they are interested in "faith healing," exorcism, or charismatic preaching. Fulfillment of vows, penitential rites like flagellation, and ritual dancing that takes place during the fiesta of Santo Niño de Cebu, are immensely popular for reasons not entirely religious.

The church does not sanction all flagellations. They become folk religious practice when the people flog and scourge themselves without the approval of the church. Flagellation in this local context takes on different forms, connotations, and meanings. Widely practiced in some Pampanga, Bulacan, Rizal, and Bicol towns, "the *disciplina* became the *penitensiya*."[29] Stripped to the waist, flagellants wear hoods crowned with branches to symbolize the crown of thorns worn by Jesus.

Filipinos practice flagellation to fulfill a vow. This is significant in lowland Philippine culture, which stresses the importance of paying of debt or

28. Dyrness, *Invitation to Cross-cultural Theology*, 89.
29. Zialcita, "Popular Interpretations of the Passion of Christ," 56.

obligation—*utang na loob*.[30] Interestingly, there is absence of the sense of sin, of having offended God, in this *penitensiya*.[31] In other words, contrition seems to be missing. It is of great significance that the ritual takes place outside the church. The power of family, community, or peer group, is more important to the flagellants than the church. In fact, the flagellant never enters the church building during his ordeal. In this ritual, the flagellant consults his families and kinsmen, but not the priests.

Another interesting departure from the church's teaching on flagellation in the Philippines is the absence of the dichotomy between soul and body. Traditional Catholic teaching like Thomas à Kempis's *The Imitation of Christ* emphasizes the primacy of spirit over body. An act of physical discipline is meant to keep the body under the control of the spirit. By mastering his carnal desires, the person will be more sensitive to promptings of the Spirit. The practice of flogging in the Philippines, however, ignores this religious principle. In fact, the participant thanks God for his good health. His bloodletting cleanses and purifies his body—*nagpapa—lakas ng katawan*.[32] In other words, the flagellant's body is renewed but not his spirit.

Our Lady of Perpetual Help

In addition to the image of the Christ, devotion to Mary is also a defining characteristic of Filipino popular piety. Seventy-five percent of the national shrines in the Philippines are dedicated to Mother Mary. Even the reformed churches, such as the Iglesia Filipina Independiente (IFI) and the Episcopal Church in the Philippines (ECP), have incorporated forms of Marian piety into their liturgy, knowing how important "Marianism" is to the local culture. Further, members of indigenous movements in the Philippines, especially Mount Banahaw in Quezon province, have also their own unique forms of devotion to Mary.[33] In all these cases, we can witness forms of Marian devotion that are adapted to the local context and more importantly, relevant to their lives, in the cities as well as in the provinces.

In this section, we will examine briefly the growth and development of the Perpetual Help Devotion, which was brought to the Philippines in 1906 by Redemptorist missionaries (*Congregatio Sanctissimi Redemptoris*—C.

30. Ibid., 59.
31. Ibid., 60.
32. Ibid.
33. Sapitula, "Marian Piety and Modernity," 400.

Ss.R) from Australia. Located in the Baclaran district of the city of Parañaque, Metro Manila, the national shrine serves as an important center for popular religion. Other parishes also have their own devotion to the Perpetual Help. In the city-state of Singapore, this devotion known as Novena is immensely popular too.

Originating in Greece, the icon of the Virgin Mary found its way to Rome from Crete toward the fifteenth century. Entrusted to the Redemptorists (an Italian congregation founded by St. Alphonsus de Ligouri in 1732) by Pope Pius IX in 1866, the icon is now displayed at the main altar of the Church of St. Alphonsus de Ligouri in Rome. Devotion to Perpetual Help takes place during the novena services at Baclaran on Wednesdays and draws a huge number of faithful to the shrine since 1948. There are also Eucharistic celebrations, the first one beginning at 5:30 a.m., followed by the novena repeated ten times and ending at 7:00 p.m. An average of 100,000 people attend the Wednesday services at the shrine.

Modern forms of popular piety sprung out in the Philippines after the Spanish colonial period when there was a "move away from religious monoculturalism that rendered the Catholic Church one actor among many others in a pluralizing public domain. At the turn of the twentieth century the 'reforming spirit' sought to upgrade Catholic practices in line with posthispanic cultural dispositions."[34] The Perpetual Help Devotion is a good example of such reforming spirit during the twentieth century, when Filipinos sought to shed the shackles of colonialism. This modern Marian devotion is different from previous Marian pieties, which were crafted in Spain.

In the early years of Spanish colonialism in the Philippines, missionaries had utilized Marian piety as a substitute for devotion to local indigenous deities. In this process of adaptation and adoption, Christianity took on a local flavor. The natives accepted Iberian Christian iconography but imbued these *larawan* (images) with *bisa* (potency).[35] In other words, it is a syncretism, a mixture of Christian and indigenous elements—the assimilation of a Christian framework in local beliefs and practices.

The church also utilized Marian devotion to reinforce Catholic values as the moral foundation of Filipino society. According to Manuel Victor J. Sapitula, "this strategy was accomplished amid the tense relations between Catholic ecclesiastical officials and the American insular government and the Catholic Church's dismay over vigorous Protestant missionary activities

---

34. Ibid., 402–3.
35. Ibid., 401.

that threatened Catholic numerical superiority." The arrival of Perpetual Help Devotion in 1906 signifies a break from previous Iberian-inspired form of Marian piety: "it epitomized a doctrinally conscious and tempered devotional heritage characteristic of posthispanic Philippine Catholicism."[36]

Coming from Australia, most of them of Anglo or Irish descent, the Redemptorists adopted an evangelization approach that was modern and independent from state control, with new insights influenced by social sciences. This was vastly different from the Spanish friars who were supported by their monarchs at a time when there was marriage between the altar and the throne. The Australian missionaries, conscious of their status as non-Spanish clergy, distinguished themselves from the Spanish friars, promoted a Marian piety that touches the heart, but also under ecclesiastical control.

Catholic piety in modern times was a strategy adopted by Rome and not a spontaneous movement developed by the masses as was commonly believed. According to Bill McSweeney, "it was a *cause* of Catholic compliance, not merely its effect and expression."[37] In other words, it is through pious practices like Perpetual Help Devotion that the church exercises control so that it has the authority to make its official teaching effective. The devotional practices at Perpetual Help Shrine include official rites such as celebration of the Eucharist, Benediction of the Sacrament, and other forms of liturgical prayers. This popular piety thus harmonizes with the Liturgy so that the faithful can participate fully in church life.

The missionary style of the Redemptorists downplays emotionalism and emphasizes doctrines in religious practices. The novena consists of established formulas of prayers, which are tools to educate the faithful on fundamental Catholic principles. The novena services also recognize the material or temporal needs of the people such as bodily healing, stability in daily life, and protection from natural calamities. This restrained Mariology also stresses the closeness of Mary as "Our Dearest Mother" or "Dear Mother of Perpetual Help."[38]

The concern for material welfare in the Perpetual Help novena prayer is consoling for people living in urban areas, and facing lots of pressure and uncertainties. This devotion resonates well with the residents in Manila with its emphasis on physical well-being, material security as well as spiritual health. This shrine also promotes an "integral evangelization" that

---

36. Ibid., 404.
37. McSweeney, *Roman Catholicism*, 38.
38. Sapitula, "Marian Piety and Modernity," 405.

seeks to integrate faith and daily practices, promotes "true devotion" that is perceived as "mission-oriented," and "socially conscious."[39] Perpetual Help Devotion is a more rationalized form of practice, very different from other localized forms of Marian piety such as devotion to Nuestra Señora de Caysasay (Batangas), Manaoag (Pangasinan), or Peñafrancia (Bicol), among others. Perpetual Help Devotion, regarded as a modern popular piety, serves to attract new generations of Catholics who are not interested in Hispanic-oriented piety from the past.

Finally, since the 1990s, many Muslim migrants from Mindanao have settled in Baclaran, where they work as vendors, capitalizing on the huge number of devotees at the shrine. This has led to encounters between Christians and Muslims, which at times causes tension and suspicion. At any rate, the Perpetual Help Shrine has emerged as a place where religious pluralism occurs in a predominantly Christian nation. Perhaps this is the place where they can learn to be tolerant and to live harmoniously under the watchful care of our Dearest Mother Mary.

Religious Imagination

David Tracy describes "imagination" as the vital vision we possess that informs our religious belief. This vision would influence our relationship with God and with one another and also our fundamental attitude towards life, be it optimistic or pessimistic, hope or despair.[40] Tracy also holds that in every great religious tradition, there is revelation that expands this vital vision through ethical, philosophical, and logical reflections. In short, religious imagination opens up new ways of being in the world as we contemplate God.

Following Tracy's idea of religious imagination, Andrew Greeley speaks about the presence of Catholic imagination in the United States, which can also be applied to the Philippines where popular piety is transmitted through families and society at large. Catholics live in an enchanted world that is filled with statues, holy water, votive candles, images of saints, religious medals, rosaries, etc. These religious paraphernalia point to a deeper sense of the sacred that Catholics perceive hiding in creation.

---

39. Ibid., 418.
40. Tracy, *The Catholic Analogical Imagination*, 235–36.

Greeley describes this Catholic imagination as "sacramental," in that reveals the presence of the divine.[41]

Such Catholic imagination corresponds with Filipino piety, which moves in the direction of vision and image. As such, this sacramental imagination flourishes throughout the islands of the Philippines with minimum doctrinal foundation. Filipinos are predisposed to accept Catholicism and the cults of the saints. In fact, the pre-Hispanic Filipinos became Christians without any resistance because they did not have to change their fundamental religious attitude.[42] Filipino Folk Catholicism may be filled with superstitious and idolatrous beliefs, but elements of Christ's message are also present in the people's faith.[43]

Popular religion, in most cases, is a genuine expression of Catholic spirituality in the Philippines and not a deviant form of Christianity. The visual and communal nature of Filipino consciousness means that their popular piety has to find expressions in visible and social forms. Thus, faith in God, acts of repentance and worship, an inner reality, must always be a public event in Filipino religious life. Solidarity is the keyword to understanding Filipino religiosity and thus, celebration of the passion of Christ—through honoring the Black Nazarene, Santo Niño, devotion to the Blessed Mother, and even flagellation— is about being together to fulfill one's personal religious duties, obligations, or vows.

Catholicism flourished in the Philippines in spite of anti-Spanish sentiments as well as fierce proselytizing by American Protestant missionaries during the late nineteenth and early twentieth centuries. Catholic piety remains embedded in the Filipino social and cultural fabric. This is an example of successful accommodation of local culture with popular Catholicism. In the next chapter, we will discuss in more detail the topic of accommodation and inculturation, with a focus on the missionary endeavors of Matteo Ricci in China.

---

41. Greeley, *The Catholic Imagination*, 1–2.
42. Gener, "The Catholic Imagination and Popular Religion," 47.
43. Dyrness, *Invitation to Cross-cultural Theology*, 104.

Chapter 4

Accommodation and Inculturation

The vast varieties of popular piety, practiced all over the world, from simple devotion to saints or to the Blessed Virgin Mary to the most elaborate processions on feast days or during the Holy Week, demonstrate that it is greatly influenced by its historical and cultural backgrounds. Many forms of popular piety have been accepted by the church throughout the ages—this is a sign that the faith has taken root and has affected people in their daily life. Popular piety is the most fundamental form of inculturation of the faith: "The encounter between the innovative dynamism of the Gospel message, and the various elements of a given culture, is affirmed in popular piety."[1]

Critical of popular piety that does not focus on the sacramental life, the Church is also aware that this kind of piety comes directly from the people, formulated in the native tongue within the framework of Catholicism. It thus calls for discernment to ensure that ideas contrary to the gospel or debased by syncretism are not allowed to creep into popular religion: "it is especially necessary to ensure that those pious exercises undergoing adaptation or inculturation retain their identity and their essential characteristics."[2]

Since popular piety is rooted in the culture of the people, this chapter attempts to demonstrate the importance of inculturation for effective evangelization. Although the term *inculturation* did not appear in the

---

1. *Directory on Popular Piety and the Liturgy*, no. 91. Some material in this chapter appeared as an article in Mong, "The legacy of Matteo Ricci and his companions" and *Accommodation and Acceptance*.

2. *Directory on Popular Piety and the Liturgy*, no. 92.

documents of Vatican II, it became an important theme when the church spoke about culture and evangelization.[3] Karl Rahner used the term *inculturation (Enkulturation)* during this period to suggest accommodation or adaptation. For John Paul II, inculturation is associated with the incarnation: "Inculturation is to be understood along the lines of the very incarnation of the Gospel within a particular culture."[4]

This chapter further examines Matteo Ricci's effort to accommodate and adapt Confucianism in propagating Christianity in China and his polemics against Buddhism. Another attempt is a critical study of Ricci's work, *The True Meaning of The Lord of Heaven*, emphasizing its strengths and weaknesses. An appreciation of native culture implies sympathetic understanding of its religions. Although Ricci was, in general, against Buddhism and Taoism, this chapter concludes that he can still be considered a pioneer in laying the foundation for interfaith relations, cultural exchanges that include inculturation.

The success of the early church in winning converts was largely due to its ability to adapt to the local cultural and social milieu. Adopting the Greco-Roman model, philosophy of Greece, and culture of Rome, in the first five centuries, Christianity became a powerful political force in Europe. Unfortunately, when the church became a dominant power, it did not feel the need to dialogue, much less to accommodate to non-Western cultures.

In more recent times, the church has been more reactive rather than active in the face of religious, social, and political upheavals such as the Reformation in the sixteenth century and the onslaught of secular ideologies such as Modernism and Marxism in the late nineteenth and early twentieth centuries. Defensive and Eurocentric, the church's teaching took refuge in medieval scholasticism. Yet, in actual fact, accommodation or inculturation is the key to the church's survival and success in evangelization.

First and foremost, to proclaim the gospel message successfully, the church must have a deep love for the culture of the people whom it wants to convert. This may sound trite, but in the past, the church had experienced painful failure because there were Western missionaries who despised the culture of the natives due to their sense of superiority, stupidity, or ignorance. Colonialism and racism were rampant in many mission territories. Rudyard Kipling (1856–1936) expressed these sentiments in his poem, "The White Man's Burden" (1899):

3. Schreiter, "Culture and inculturation in the church," 18.
4. Doyle, "The Concept of Inculturation in Roman Catholicism," 7–8.

> TAKE up the White Man's burden—
>   Send forth the best ye breed—
> Go bind your sons to exile
>   To serve your captives' need;
> To wait in heavy harness,
>   On fluttered folk and wild—
> Your new-caught, sullen peoples,
> Half-devil and half-child.

Unfortunately, this was the attitude that many missionaries consciously or unconsciously adopted when dealing with the locals. Many of them were unwitting tools of Western imperialism, ignorant of indigenous cultures.

Effective Evangelization

To evangelize effectively and realistically, the church must understand the culture of the people. This begins with cultivating a genuine love for the people. Evangelization should not be just based on planning strategy or any scientific approach but on understanding and love that come from the heart. The church must attempt to learn and to discern how the culture of a particular people operates. It is also important for the church to know the direction in which the culture is heading rather than looking merely at the past.[5] Challenged by globalization, relentless capitalism, communism, and secularism, evangelization must be carried out against the backdrop of an established culture.

When the church proclaims the gospel, people accept it in faith only when "it becomes incarnate among them and assumes their cultures."[6] A close bond is thus forged between the faithful and their culture, and the faith that is transmitted by the church, is lived out in the daily lives of the people. The establishment of the kingdom of God is based on elements borrowed from the material and intellectual traditions of the people:

> ... the kingdom which the Gospel proclaims is lived by men who are profoundly linked to a culture, and the building up of the kingdom cannot avoid borrowing the elements of human culture or cultures. Though independent of cultures, the Gospel and evangelization are not necessarily incompatible with them; rather they

---

5. Eagleson and Scharper, eds., *Puebla and Beyond*, nos. 397–398.
6. Ibid., no. 400.

are capable of permeating them all without becoming subject to any one of them.[7]

Cultures are not vacuums without values and the evangelization work of the church should not destroy native cultures. Rather the church should consolidate and strengthen those values that would in turn contribute to the growth of the "seeds of the Word" embedded in the cultures: "We know likewise that the world and history are filled with 'seeds of the Word'; is it not therefore an illusion to claim to bring the Gospel where it already exists in the seeds that the Lord Himself has sown?"[8]

Further, the church is even more interested in assuming the Christian values found in people who are already evangelized and who have lived out those values in their own cultural expressions. The local church therefore must make an effort to adapt itself and to translate the gospel message into the "anthropological idiom and symbols of the culture in which it immerses itself."[9] Pope Paul VI wrote: "Evangelization loses much of its force and effectiveness if it does not take into consideration the actual people to whom it is addressed, if it does not use their language, their signs and symbols, if it does not answer the questions they ask, and if it does not have an impact on their concrete life."[10]

Thus the church, "living in various circumstances in the course of time, has used the discoveries of different cultures so that in her preaching she might spread and explain the message of Christ to all nations, that she might examine it and more deeply understand it, that she might give it better expression in liturgical celebration and in the varied life of the community of the faithful."[11]

It is also the church's duty to denounce the presence of sins, especially idolatry, in human conduct. Denouncing all forms of idolatry, the church purifies and exorcises the evil that is present in the culture. This happens when values that a culture possesses are perceived as absolute when in reality they are not. Evangelization requires that the church teaches people to abandon their false concept of God, their unnatural behavior, their exploitation and manipulation of other people, etc. The specific task of evangelization is to proclaim Christ. This, however, does not mean that cultures must

7. Pope Paul VI, *Evangelii Nuntiandi*, no. 20.
8. Ibid., no. 80.
9. Eagleson and Scharper, eds., *Puebla and Beyond*, no. 404.
10. Pope Paul VI, *Evangelii Nuntiandi*, no. 63.
11. Pope Paul VI, *Gaudium et spes*, no. 58

be subordinated to "ecclesiastical regime."[12] It does mean that people have to accept the spiritual lordship of Christ. Through evangelization, cultures will be renovated, elevated, and perfected by the power of the risen Christ.

Accommodation

As a result of the Protestant Reformation during the sixteenth century, the Catholic Church began to strengthen its structure and impose the Roman Rite, putting a brake to further attempts at inculturation. With the missionary expansion that took place during the eighteenth century, the Catholic Reform movement exported the Roman Liturgy and organizational structure to the other parts of the world where the gospel message was proclaimed. Thus in those mission territories, the relationship between Liturgy and popular piety was similar to that in Europe during the sixteenth and seventeenth centuries. In fact, it was "more accentuated" because of the fear of syncretism. In other words, "the Liturgy retained a Roman character and hence remained, at least partially, extraneous to autochthonous culture. The question of inculturation was practically never raised, partly because of the fear of negative consequence for the faith."[13] Church authorities feared popular piety might be exposed to the danger of religious syncretism. In this respect, I would like to mention the special effort in accommodation made by the Italian Jesuit, Matteo Ricci, in relation to Chinese culture.

It should be noted that "accommodation" as a method of evangelization was as old as Christianity itself. The early Church Fathers sought to convey the Christian message using categories adapted from Hellenistic culture. It was so successful that the church made it an exclusive norm. We are not sure how far Ricci was aware of this patristic period of inculturation and how far he was improvising. But by adapting Christianity to the Chinese culture, Ricci was simply following the footsteps of Justin, Athenagoras, and Clement of Alexandria. Justin said, "Whatever men have uttered right belongs to us Christians." Further, the theory of *logos* claims that "whatever either lawgivers or philosophers uttered well, they elaborated by finding and contemplating some part of the Word."[14] Nonetheless, there is no evidence that Ricci had studied patristic literature seriously in either Rome or Goa.

12. Eagleson and Scharper, eds., *Puebla and Beyond*, no. 407.
13. *Directory on Popular Piety and the Liturgy*, no. 43.
14. Rule, "Jesuit and Confucian," 107.

During the Ming period, Confucianism was the best vehicle to transmit the Christian faith among the Chinese intellectual elite. Both Confucianism and Christianity are still very much alive today, and they can enhance and illuminate each other as Paul S. Chung has argued: "Confucianism as a living tradition becomes a catalyst in bringing Christian faith to the project of ethical humanism, and Confucian social ontology of *ren* 仁 and politics of rectification become an interlocutor for Christian theology to be more socially engaged and amenable to reconciliation, justice, and recognition of the other."[15] It is to Ricci's credit that he eventually refrained from criticizing non-Christian beliefs by focusing on weaving the Christian values to the ethics and virtues in the tradition of the Great Sage, Master Kong.

Religious Intolerance

Francis Xavier was the first missionary who attempted to enter China during the Ming dynasty but without success. He died in Shangchuan, an island ten kilometers off the mainland, while waiting in vain for permission to enter China proper. It was left to Matteo Ricci to take up this challenging task again. Accepted for the mission, he and his Jesuit companions departed Rome on May 18, 1577. On the way to the Far East, Ricci stopped in Goa, a city along the west coast of India, to continue his studies for the priesthood at the Jesuit College of St. Paul.

Goa was a Portuguese colony that had strict surveillance over religious orthodoxy. This charge was given to a local tribunal of the Inquisition, headed by Bartolomeu da Fonseca, who had boasted of burning many heretics. In this Portuguese outpost, Ricci had witnessed the worst of religious intolerance when seventeen were burned at stake after being forced to walk through the streets in tunics impregnated with sulphur. Many of them were Jews forced to embrace Christianity *(conversos)* but were suspected of secret adherence to Judaism.[16] In spite of the diversity of people in Goa with a large number of Hindus and Muslims, the Portuguese only allowed the practice of Catholicism in the city.

Besides the burning of heretics in Goa by the Portuguese Inquisition, Ricci came to know that the Hindu and Muslim populations were forced to accept Christianity. In fact, Portuguese soldiers burned down the city's Hindu temples in 1540. Christian converts were required to abandon their

---

15. Chung, "Christian-Confucian dialogue in construction of cultural reality," 55.
16. See Spence, *The Memory Palace of Matteo Ricci*, 110–11.

Accommodation and Inculturation

castes and customs, and to adopt Portuguese names and manner of dressing. These two events must have shocked and scandalized Ricci. Later, he would receive news that his Jesuit companions including Rodolfo Aquaviva, head of the mission at Salcette near Goa, were killed by the natives because of hatred for the priests in connection to the destructions of their temples by Portuguese authorities.[17] Obviously, contempt for local religions on the part of the missionaries would only lead to conflict and violence. Ricci would learn this quickly.

Experiencing the brutalities and cruelties of the Portuguese colonizers must have been a rude awakening for the young Ricci: he "found himself in that world of blurred boundaries between the sacred and the secular, where religion was mixed up with trafficking, war, coercion, and death."[18] It was certainly a far cry from what he had learned and expected regarding the mission while he was a student at the Roman College. These horrifying experiences of religious intolerance of the Portuguese rulers in India in addition to the tropical heat took a toll on him. Ricci became very ill and was transferred to Cochin, a town south of Goa. For nearly a year, he stayed in Cochin, continued his study of theology, and taught Latin and Greek to the local pupils. He was ordained to the priesthood in Cochin and celebrated his first mass on July 26, 1580.

From the beginning Ricci had stood firmly on certain principles regarding the mission and the role of the church. He was not afraid to speak out and oppose his superiors when he discovered the approaches/strategies adopted in the mission territory were wrong. The Jesuit authorities had forbidden ethnic Indians studying for the priesthood from attending courses on philosophy and theology for fear that they would be too proud of their learning and thus refuse to work with the poor. This was an ill-founded policy, Ricci thought. He questioned why European novices were allowed to be educated in the entire syllabus while the Indians were forbidden. Further, he argued that not all European priests put their knowledge to good use. A staunch defender of the role of knowledge and culture in evangelization, Ricci insisted that all priests, Europeans as well as Asians, must be well trained. Otherwise the laity would be deprived of competent spiritual guides. Besides, having ill-equipped priests among the natives would incur hatred and might encourage superficial conversions.

---

17. Fontana, *Matteo Ricci: A Jesuit in the Ming Court*, 25.
18. Ibid., 24.

Thus we see Ricci championing the rights of the Indian Jesuits to have the same intellectual formation as their European counterparts. In spite of its international outlook, the Society of Jesus was reluctant to recruit the natives, believing that they did not possess the required intellectual abilities. In fact, Ricci belonged to the minority of Jesuits who supported the admission of Indians into the Company.[19]

Ricci's protest was a courageous step for a member of an Order that emphasized absolute obedience. Described as a person who was "emotional yet disciplined, obedient yet critical," Ricci stood by his conviction regarding the importance of knowledge in winning converts.[20] He had observed at close quarters how the coercions of the Portuguese soldiers in Goa regarding religion as well as trade would only cause fear and hatred. Ricci was determined to adopt a totally different policy as laid down by his mentor, Alessandro Valignano. Thus, in his plan to convert the Chinese people, Ricci adopted the *modo soave*—the gentle method—when dealing with his hosts' culture.

Alessandro Valignano

Born in 1539 to a noble family in Chieti, Alessandro was a well-built and impressive person. Unlike Ricci, who entered the Society as a young fervent novice straight from college, Valignano had studied law at the University of Padua. Later, he was arrested and imprisoned for allegedly assaulting a woman. Released from prison thanks to the intervention of Cardinal Borromeo, Valignano then joined the Jesuits at San Andrea. As mentioned earlier, he was Matteo Ricci's novice master in the novitiate. As Jesuit Visitor to the Far East, Valignano was convinced that missionaries should learn the language and culture of the country in which they work. They needed to learn the native way of life, to adapt to its customs, and respect its traditions unless it contradicted Christian morality. Generally known as cultural accommodation, this missionary policy was considered avant-garde at that time and rejected by Rome during the "Chinese Rites" Controversy.

According to Pasquale D'Elia, the policy of Valignano was not to "Europeanize" the natives but to evangelize within the local cultural context, adopting those traditions and social customs that were compatible with

---

19. Hsia, *A Jesuit in the Forbidden City*, 49.
20. Ibid., 50.

Christian teachings.[21] Of course, the Jesuits' Far East mission is not just a simple tale of accommodation. A complex set of factors, arising from both European and Chinese circumstances, including Chinese cultural imperative, dictated how the task of evangelization was to be carried out. By and large, the Jesuits in the Far East relied on evangelizing methods and pastoral practices employed by European Catholics, which include the learning of indigenous languages and confronting other faiths.[22]

In spite of past failures of foreign missionaries propagating the faith in China, Valignano was determined to succeed because he was convinced that China was "a great and noble country inhabited by people of lively intellect given to study and governed with peace and prudence."[23] Impressed by the achievements of the Japanese and Chinese people, especially in their literature, politics, and philosophy, Valignano decided to make cultural accommodation the foundation of the Jesuits' missionary enterprise. Jean-Paul Wiest claims Valignano was the one "who master-minded this new approach, which was based on the concept of a multipolar world whose center was no longer Europe."[24] Matteo Ricci was specially chosen to pioneer Valignano's new missionary project, which no longer looked upon Europe as the exclusive model for Christian civilization. It is important to note that the policy of cultural accommodation was not uniformly practiced throughout the Society of Jesus.

As a visitor in the Far East, Valignano was able to secure some degree of independence for the Jesuits in China. He recruited missionaries who were not influenced by the militant Christianity practiced by the Spaniards and Portuguese. An Italian noble himself, Valignano knew that the Italian Jesuits were not influenced by this crusade mentality, but were imbued with the spirit of the Italian Renaissance and intellectually competent to deal with the Chinese literati. Hence, the model for Catholic Mission in the Far East was Italian—"the cultural golden age of a specifically Catholic humanism."[25]

---

21. Fontana, *Matteo Ricci*, 27.
22. Brockey, *Journey to the East*, 406.
23. Fontana, *Matteo Ricci*, 27.
24. Wiest, "Matteo Ricci," 17.
25. Ibid.

Cultural Accommodation

The first step in cultural accommodation is to learn the language of the natives. Arriving in Macau, a Portuguese colony, in 1582, Ricci started learning Chinese in preparation for his great work in mainland China. Although he was well trained in learning new languages, Ricci found Chinese difficult because it was completely different from any of the European languages he had studied. Gifted with a fantastic memory, eventually he became fluent in the language after much toil and effort. In fact, Ricci never stopped studying Chinese language, history, and philosophy in order to be on par with the Confuciucian literati. To convert them to the Christian faith, Ricci realized that he must be their intellectual equal. The relentless effort to study Chinese was also motivated by his plan to write a new catechism to replace the older text by Michele Ruggieri. To do this, Ricci needed to have a better grasp of Chinese philosophy.

Aware that all educated Chinese had studied the Confucius Analects, Ricci was determined to study this philosophy carefully so that he could dialogue with Chinese scholars on an equal footing. Confucian philosophy consists of ethical and political principles, but without a metaphysical foundation. It presents a society that is hierarchical, and emphasizes the importance of rituals and culture as a means of human improvement. In fact, during the time of Ricci, the basis of Chinese centralized and bureaucratic government was Confucian ideology.

During Ricci's time there was a debate between whether Confucianism was a philosophy or a religion. Julia Ching observes that, "From his own account of spiritual evolution, it might also be inferred that Confucius was a religious man, a believer in Heaven, a personal God, a man who sought to understand and follow Heaven's will."[26] Ching's definition of religion includes a consciousness of a dimension of transcendence that "I perceive as having been present in Confucianism from the very beginning, even though this has not always referred to a belief in a personal deity. . . . [T]he very insistence upon the priority of the way of Heaven, and the quest itself for the discovery and fulfillment of such within the way of man, point to a movement toward self-transcendence." Thus Confucianism "remains religious at its core on account of its spiritual teachings of sagehood or

---

26. Küng and Ching, *Christianity and Chinese Religions*, 67.

self-transcendence."²⁷ Further, if we consider religion to be a quest for ultimate meaning in life, then Confucianism can also be regarded as a religion.

Regarding the study of Confucius's thought, Ricci distinguished Classical Confucianism from Neo-Confucianism because the latter he thought was contradictory to fundamental Christian teaching. Like most philosophies, Confucianism had been revised and interpreted in different manners over the centuries. During the Ming Dynasty, Neo-Confucianism incorporated elements of Buddhist and Taoist teachings. Ricci, however, did not accept this interpretation with its emphasis on a supreme principle (*taiji* 太極) as the origin and foundation of all things. He favored Classical Confucianism, which spoke of the "Lord on High" (*Shangdi* 上帝), a personal god quite similar to the Christian understanding.²⁸ Thus Ricci's preference for Classical Confucianism is based on its purported compatibility with Christianity. Neo-Confucian scholars, on the other hand, adapted the teachings of Confucius and Mencius according to their own historical context and as a particular response to the challenge of Mahāyāna Buddhism, which some scholars believe to be parallel to Christianity.

At the end of 1594, Ricci had produced the first Latin paraphrase of Confucian works, *The Four Books of Confucianism*, accompanied by commentaries. Ricci found great similarities between Confucius's morality and the principles of Western ethics, and also a close affinity between Chinese philosophy and Stoicism. He regarded Confucius as "another Seneca" comparable to the great classical writers in Europe.²⁹ Emphasizing the common ground between Christianity and the Confucian classics, Ricci told his Chinese friends that "the law of God was in conformity with the natural light [of reason] and with what their first sages taught in their books."³⁰ A wily person, Ricci "deliberately presented his precepts in the Confucian style, emphasizing the importance of self-improvement in the knowledge that this was one of the most important virtues taught by Confucius, and seeking to show that this could come about through learning to worship the Lord of Heaven."³¹ Thus Ricci regarded Confucianism as natural law and not a religion. Its emphasis on the principle of filial piety reviewed to him the importance of morality, ethics and not simply the worship of idols.

27. Ibid., 89.
28. Fontana, *Matteo Ricci*, 106.
29. Ibid., 105.
30. Wiest, "Matteo Ricci," 19.
31. Fontana, *Matteo Ricci*, 226.

Needless to say, the study and translation of the *Four Books* helped Ricci integrate into Chinese society and earned the respect and admiration of the literati. It was the first time they had seen a "barbarian" knowledgeable in Confucius classics. Li Madou (利瑪竇), as the Chinese called Matteo Ricci, was turning into a (*shidafu* 士大夫—Chinese scholar) and was regarded by them as their equal. This achievement also qualified Ricci to dress like a Confucian scholar. This was considered the most practical step towards "accommodation." The adoption of the dress and way of life of the literati was accepted from the beginning of the Jesuit mission.

The True Meaning of the Lord of Heaven

Upon the advice of Alessandro Valignano, Ricci began to work on his catechism, entitled *The True Meaning of the Lord of Heaven*. It was an effective strategy to win converts among the Chinese elites as the literati valued written words more than spoken ones. The first catechism was written by Ruggieri, revised by Ricci, and published in 1584. But Valignano considered Ruggier's work inadequate because of the Buddhist terms he used to express Christian thoughts. In (co)writing this volume, Ricci's aim was to reflect Confucianism and refute Buddhism in presenting Christianity.

Confucius stressed moral self-improvement, and hence, Ricci's objective in his catechism was to develop the nature of self-cultivation. Ricci argued that the person who seeks to improve himself has to worship the Lord of Heaven. Confucian teaching emphasizes the relationship between heaven and human beings with little reference to God, and thus Ricci had to search for current philosophical ideas to support his thesis on God and man. Critical of the nihilistic doctrines in Taoism and the pantheistic thought in Buddhism and Neo-Confucianism, Ricci also condemned the superstitious practices prevalent among the Chinese.[32] He wished to convince the Chinese that ancient Confucianism was compatible with Christianity, but before it was contaminated by Buddhist and Taoist elements resulting in a Neo-Confucian interpretation. Citing the classical texts of Confucianism selectively, the Jesuit interprets them to suit his purpose.

In this work, Ricci first focuses on the existence of one God, the creator of heaven and earth. Repudiating the Buddhist and Taoist teaching of *Taiji*, a form of energy regarded by Neo-Confucianism as the origin of the universe, Ricci emphasizes the Christian understanding of a personal

---

32. Ricci, *The True Meaning of The Lord of Heaven*, 22–23.

Accommodation and Inculturation

God. He begins by setting forth the proofs for the existence of God, arguing that God created the universe and all things in it. Then he uses classical Confucianism to refute the Taoist concept of *Wu* (無) or "Non-Being" and the Buddhist concept of *K'ung* (空) or "voidness."[33] Going back to the history of Chinese culture, Ricci attempts to show the idea of one personal god—*Shangdi*—the Lord of Heaven—present in ancient Chinese classics. In other words, the Chinese understanding of *Tian* (天-Heaven) actually refers to the Christian God, the Father Almighty.

The Chinese believed that the universe was one single organism, but Ricci emphasized the difference between human and divine nature, and claimed the existence of the soul as a spiritual entity separated from the body. This duality between spirit and body, however, was foreign to Chinese thought. Ricci's catechism holds that humans are different from animals in that the former possess reason.

Part Two begins a refutation of the Buddhist doctrine of transmigration. Ricci also criticizes the Buddhist prohibition of killing nonhuman living things and teaches the real meaning of fasting. He presents the Christian understanding of heaven and hell, and emphasizes the ability of human beings to choose between good and evil on the basis of reason. Ricci also treats the question of human nature, its goodness and sinfulness. Then he proceeds to the worship of God and how believers should practice self-cultivation. He then discusses celibacy and its relation to filial piety. Ricci did not discuss in depth God's revelation in history and this led some scholars to view this work more like a "pre-evangelical dialogue" rather than a catechism.[34] Naturally, people who have read this book and desired baptism need to be further instructed in the faith.

It is ironical that Buddhism, which Ricci and his companions sought to displace, was the very religion that they had borrowed much of their religious concepts. For example, the term, "Lord of Heaven," used to describe the Christian God, turned out to be a deity in Buddhist scriptures. Even the term *T'ein-t'ang* (天堂 or "Heaven") was used by the Buddhists as the equivalent of the Sanskrit *Devaloka* or "mansions of the gods." In Buddhist cosmology, the heavens were located "between the earth and the *Brahmalokus*," or "mansions or heavens of Brahma." Hell or *Di-yü* (地獄) was the Buddhist equivalent of the Sanskrit *naraka*. *Mo Kuei*, the term Christians used to designate the devil, comes from the Sanskrit *Māra*, the

33. Ibid., 23.
34. Ibid., 25.

tempter of Buddha. In other words, the term Christians chose to designate Satan was derived from Buddhism. Although the philosophy Ricci expresses in this work is based on St. Thomas Aquinas, he accepts the Buddhist term *ling-hun*, which means "spirit."[35]

Ricci uses the word *Sheng* (聖) for "holy," "sacred" and "saint." As a noun, *Sheng* refers to a holy person or a saint. The word gives the Chinese a sense of awe in the religious sense. However, the concept of *sheng* has no exact Christian equivalent. In the Christian context, the apposite of "saint" is "sinner" and the opposite of "holy" is "profane." But in Chinese, the opposite of *sheng* is "ignorance." The emphasis here is on moral self-cultivation with no reference to divine assistance.[36] In Ricci's time, the *sheng* in China were persons of cultural achievement from the past who attained wisdom, understanding, and cultivated virtues, in other word, a sage. Ricci also introduces the term *sheng-shen* (聖神, "sage and spiritual") for saint.[37] The search for suitable equivalents of Christian terms was indeed challenging and difficult for Ricci because the understanding of the nature of religion is different between the East and the West.

As we can see, in *The True Meaning of The Lord of Heaven* Matteo Ricci attempts to connect Christianity with Confucianism. Paul S. Chung describes Ricci's strategy as follows: he portrays Catholic doctrines as a complement to Confucianism and at the same time, he believes Catholic doctrines transcend and transform Confucius's teaching. Ricci also revises Catholic doctrines to make them more compatible with Confucian principles.[38]

Reception of Ricci's Work

It was reported that the emperor K'ang-hsi (康熙, 1662–1723) read the book, was impressed by the content, and issued the edict of toleration in March, 1692.[39] As a result of this publication, many Chinese scholars came to accept that Christianity was compatible with Confucianism. Ricci's book emphasized self-cultivation, and equated God with the Confucian concept of *Shangdi*, thus proving that elements of Catholicism could be found in

35. Ibid., 35–36.
36. Ibid., 37.
37. Ibid., 38.
38. Chung, "Christian-Confucian dialogue in construction of cultural reality," 61.
39. Ricci, *The True Meaning of The Lord of Heaven*, 39.

ancient Chinese classics.[40] In other words, Catholicism could complement Confucianism.

Ricci's catechism, though popular with some Chinese literati, was not without adverse criticism. Negative reactions came from within the Roman Catholic Church, from Protestant missionaries, from the Buddhists, Neo-Confucians, and also orthodox Confucians. Many Christians were against identifying *Shangdi* with the Judeo-Christian God and other Chinese terms for key Christian concepts. Jacques Gernet speaks of the incommensurability between Western and Eastern concepts, the radical difference between European and Chinese languages associated with different worldviews. He writes: "The missionaries, just like the Chinese literate elites, were the unconscious bearers of a whole civilization. The reason why they so often came up against difficulties of translation is that different languages express, through different logics, different visions of the world and man."[41] Thus the Jesuits had to struggle in bridging the "mental frameworks"—for example trying to find similarities between Chinese heaven and the Sovereign on High, and the biblical concept of God. Further, unlike Western philosophy, Eastern thinking tends to deny any opposition between self and the world, the mind and the body, the divine and the cosmic. In Chinese thoughts, the sensible is not separated from the rational; the spiritual substance is not distinct from the material. The Chinese cannot conceive of a world of eternal truths separated from the visible world of appearances.[42]

Attacks from Three Fronts

Criticism of Ricci's writings came from three fronts: the scientific, the political, and the philosophical-theological. On the scientific front, it was obvious from the writings that Ricci considered China to be scientifically and technologically backward. But Roger Hart argues that the Jesuits and their collaborators could not have believed in the superiority of Western science because the Jesuits themselves had appropriated many of their mathematical concepts from Chinese mathematical treatises.[43] On the political front, there was a fear that the Jesuits were actually forerunners of European armies preparing to invade China.

40. Ibid., 40.
41. Hart, *Imagined Civilizations*, 54.
42. Ibid.
43. Ibid., 260.

On the philosophical-theological front, there were three points. First, there were no hostile reactions from the Taoists as most of its adherents were drawn from the lower class with little education to understand the profundity of Ricci's writings. Second, by the end of the Ming Dynasty, Buddhism had evolved and became infused with elements from Confucianism and Taoism. Few Buddhists upheld Buddhism in its purest form. In fact, pure Buddhism does not exist. The same could be said for Confucianism. Confucianism infused with Buddhist and Taoist ideas evolved into Neo-Confucianism, a form of philosophical and religious syncretism that became very popular in the late Ming period.[44] For Buddhism to survive in China, it had to accommodate to Confucianism. In the same way, for Christianity to survive, it too had to accommodate to Confucianism. Thus, Ricci's slogan, "Draw close to Confucianism and repudiate Buddhism," could only evoke furious reactions from Buddhist quarters.

The most violent objection to Ricci's works came from orthodox Confucians. They rejected the idea that Confucianism needs to be augmented by Catholicism for its own enhancement. Adopting the Neo-Confucian position, these Confucian traditionalists slammed the affirmation of *The True Meaning of the Lord of Heaven* that "The Supreme Ultimate, being principle, cannot be the source of all creation." One of the critics called Ricci "a traitor and usurper and a rebel against Confucius . . . By destroying the Supreme Ultimate the demon Ricci destroyed the Mean."[45] Ricci's teaching on Chinese theism, doctrine of the soul, the incarnation, human nature, heaven, and hell, all came under severe scrutiny. The critics were able to prove that Ricci and his companions were ignorant of the finer distinctions of Chinese philosophy.

Recent scholars have discovered that Ricci did not have an adequate understanding of the key concepts and historical context of the various schools of Chinese philosophy at that time. He appeared not to have grasped correctly the Taoist *Wu*, the Buddhist *K'ung*, and the Neo-Confucianist *T'ai-chi*. Some scholars believe that the *Wu* of Taoism and the *K'ung* of Mahāyāna Buddhism resemble the Christian understanding of God in *via negativa*—the "negative" approach to divine reality or the apophatic tradition in Orthodox theology.[46] This is only one example of the compatibility between Christianity and Buddhism and Taoism. Other

44. Ricci, *The True Meaning of The Lord of Heaven*, 44.
45. Ibid., 45.
46. Ibid., 47.

concepts like *T'ai-chi, Li,* and *Ch' i* found in Neo-Confucianism can be extended to explain the three persons of the Trinity. Unfortunately, trapped in the scholastic framework, Ricci could not examine these terms within their original thought systems. He saw only superficial similarities while the deeper meanings of the Chinese terms escaped him.[47]

Ricci's new catechism was interpreted as a betrayal to both Christianity and Confucianism. For some Christians, Ricci seems to have sacrificed Christian truth in favor of traditional Chinese thoughts, and for the orthodox Confucians, vice versa. The works of Ricci prompted Rome to take several decisions, which included the prohibition of Catholics to venerate both their ancestors and Confucius. On the positive side, it led to heated debates and discussions in Western intellectual circles as to whether ancient Chinese thought resembled Christian teaching. These debates and discourses became channels for Chinese thoughts to be known in Europe especially during the Age of the Enlightenment, and thus, promoted dialogue between the East and the West.

Till today, some Christians believe that the policy of accommodation was a distortion of Christianity. One critic claimed that "Ricci limited himself to teaching pure deism . . . he mentioned neither Trinity, nor the Incarnation, nor the Redemption . . . It is probable that his Chinese friends saw in it only a special kind of Buddhism." Others were more harsh and described Ricci as "an unprincipled opportunist." One Catholic critic writes: "Ricci was . . . ignorant of the first principles of theology. Being more of a politician than a theologian, he discovered the secret of remaining peacefully in China." Ricci's respect for Chinese culture was interpreted as anti-Christian: "He disfigured [Christianity] by a faithful mixture of pagan superstitions, adopting the sacrifices offered to Confucius and ancestors . . . ."[48]

Nonetheless, one should not be too harsh in judging Ricci. Indeed, to judge someone in the sixteenth century with the standards of the twenty-first century is not helpful in getting a fair assessment. Besides, when Ricci wrote *The True Meaning of the Lord of Heaven*, he had been in China for less than twenty years, and thus one cannot expect him to have a thorough grasp of the richness and beauty of Chinese thoughts. Schooled in the scholastic tradition, his attitude towards non-Christian religions was bound to be negative or even hostile. Ricci favored Confucianism because

---

47. Ibid., 48.
48. Young, *East-west Synthesis*, 24.

he did not regard it as a religion competing with Christianity, but a pagan philosophy like Aristotle's, which was used by St. Thomas Aquinas to expound the Catholic faith. Ricci's understanding of Confucianism, however, was faulty for he did not take into account the historical development of this philosophy. This led him to reject Neo-Confucianism.[49] Ricci believed in pristine Confucianism, which in fact does not exist.

A Bridge

The True Meaning of the Lord of Heaven is the first attempt by a Western scholar to present Christianity dressed in Confucian robes, as it were. It anticipated the teaching of Vatican II (1962–1965) in expressing the Christian faith within the local context, according to the specific culture in which the gospel is preached. Pope John Paul II writes: "And just as the Fathers of the Church had done centuries before in the encounter between the Gospel of Jesus Christ and Greco-Roman culture, Father Ricci made this insight the basis of his patient and far-sighted work of inculturation of the faith in China, in the constant search for a common ground of understanding with the intellectuals of that great land."[50] Hence, Matteo Ricci's merit lay above all in the sphere of inculturation.

As Confucian values were deeply ingrained in Chinese society, Ricci rightly believed that these values would not be displaced by Christianity. Besides, a Christian nation could also be a Confucian one—there was no contradiction. Some of his writings showed that he was "converted" to Confucianism in the process of teaching Christianity.[51] Perhaps Ricci's so-called conversion to Confucianism revealed his adeptness in inculturation as taught by Vatican II. It was his genius to construct a synthesis of Eastern and Western values, like a bridge to join two distinct continents. Europe and China will be like two worlds separated by an enormous distance, but will mutually instruct and enlighten each other.

Ricci's policy of accommodation and inculturation had also sparked off the so-called Rites Controversy. In the following chapter, we will examine the fine line between superstition and true worship, and the debate regarding superstition and the cult of ancestor veneration in China

---

49. Ricci, *The True Meaning of The Lord of Heaven*, 50.

50. Message of His Holiness Pope John Paul II for the Fourth Centenary of the arrival in Beijing of the great missionary and scientist Matteo Ricci.

51. Young, *East-west Synthesis*, 43.

Chapter 5

Superstition and Piety

Attending mass regularly, laying flowers at the feet of the statue of the Blessed Virgin Mary, lighting candles in church, and taking part in a public procession carrying relics of saints are acts of devotion and faith. It does not matter if the individual is well versed in Scripture or knows nothing more than that God will always keep his word to the faithful.

Popular piety is thus perceived as an appropriation of doctrine by the common people, and even by clerics, too. Such acts take place among believers from all walks of life as they respond to the church's teachings and practice them in ways based on the believers' own interpretation. These practices are most commonly associated with devotion to the Blessed Virgin Mary, veneration of saints and their shrines, and a strong belief in miracles and signs. The practices are widespread in many countries in the developed world and the Third World. And they are not restricted to simple folks; many devout priests and thoughtful, educated laypeople have also embraced popular piety with enthusiasm.

What makes a religious practice popular is its usefulness and practicality. Popular religious practices help people cope emotionally with life's seismic events such as birth, major illness, and dying. Nevertheless, the Church is concerned that some of the practices are derived from superstition, false beliefs, or ritualistic magic. This is because popular religion touches the heart rather than the head. Doctrines serve to nourish the mind; but people need more tangible signs from God to help them survive the difficulties and hardship that life presents. Associated with church authorities, doctrines become popular only when they have meaningful applications in day-to-day living.[1]

Popular piety also reveals the longing that the poor and humble have for God; further, their patience, generosity and willingness to sacrifice for the sake of their faith. These various Christian cult-like expressions, both private and public, arose from a specific culture or people, according to the *Directory on Popular Piety and the Liturgy*, issued by the Congregation for Divine Worship and the Discipline of the Sacraments in 2001.

While acknowledging the importance of popular piety in the life of the faithful, the *Directory* warns of the negative impact to which such devotion may lead. In this warning, the *Directory* emphasizes the primacy and preeminence of the Liturgy as "every liturgical celebration, because it is an action of Christ the Priest and of His Body, which is the church, is a sacred action surpassing all others."[2] In other words, no spiritual exercises of the church can be as effective as the Eucharistic celebration. We should also avoid thinking that because the Liturgy is official Church worship, it is therefore not "popular" when compared with popular piety. The Church thus encourages people to participate fully in the celebration of the Liturgy, which is obligatory for all Christians, while types of devotions and popular piety are optional.

Mindful of Christians from other traditions, popular piety as a true treasure of the people of God must possess an ecumenical spirit. The *Directory* stresses the anthropological spirit that should inspire popular piety; it has to take seriously the symbols and expressions of the specific culture from which the devotion arises. It has to maintain a constant dialogue with contemporary culture so that popular piety does not become obsolete. Besides asserting the primacy and distinctiveness of the Liturgy, the *Directory* insists that popular piety must always be in harmony with it. This is because the Liturgy forms the core of our worship.

This chapter discusses some of the salient points in the *Directory*, highlighting the tension between official Church worship and popular devotion. While acknowledging the Church's need to control the practices of popular devotion, we examine the fine line between superstition and genuine piety by comparing the thoughts of Erasmus and Newman. Grounded in Scripture and infused with the Holy Spirit, popular piety must not be contaminated by superstition, magic, or animism. It must be imbued with a

---

1. Ryan, "Some reflections on theology and popular piety," 964–65.
2. *Directory on Popular Piety and the Liturgy*, no. 11.

liturgical perception that reflects the Christian mysteries. However, superstitious beliefs are imbedded in many indigenous cultures and they sometimes may serve as an impetus towards true piety, as Newman suggested.

An important aspect of popular piety is the cult involving the memorial of the dead. Unfortunately, the *Directory* provides little guidance on the practices of popular piety towards the dead. In fact, Peter Phan laments "the Directory's narrow focus on *suffrage* for the dead, while concentrating on what the church does *for* the dead, neglects many aspects of the cult *in honour* of the dead."[3] This chapter will therefore examine the Chinese cult of ancestor veneration in the context of the so-called Rites Controversy. The cult of ancestors is an important and challenging aspect of popular piety, not only in Chinese society but in many other Asian and African societies, too.

Domination of Roman Rite

The Catholic Reform movement served to strengthen the structure and unity of the Roman Rite, which spread to other countries through missionary expansion in the eighteenth century. In other words, the Liturgy maintained a strong Roman character because there was no attempt at inculturation for fear of religious syncretism in places where Gospel values were not deeply rooted. Nonetheless, in places promoted by the missionaries, popular piety reflecting the local culture flourished.

In the twentieth century, we witnessed local cultic expression that originated from the various ethnic groups' initiatives related to miracles and apparitions. These devotions were incorporated into the Liturgy eventually. A significant phenomenon during this period was the establishment of Marian shrines. The relationship between popular piety and the Liturgy, the *Directory* highlights, must be viewed in the context of liturgical revival and the flourishing of popular piety.

Striking a balance

In the modern age, it was Pope Pius X (1903–1914) who was instrumental in bringing the Liturgy closer to the people by encouraging active participation in the mysteries of our faith. He drew a clear distinction between

---

3. Phan, "Suffrage for the Dead," 139.

Liturgy and popular piety, dispelling confusion between the two forms of cultic expression. In the context of this liturgical movement, while upholding the preeminence of the Liturgy, some began to see popular piety as a kind of abuse or superstition. The *Directory* states: "In their efforts to restore the purity of divine worship, they took as their ideal the Liturgy of the early centuries of the church, and consequently radically rejected any form of popular piety deriving from the Middles Ages or the post-Tridentine period."[4]

Unfortunately, in this outright rejection, the critics failed to note the validity of some forms of popular devotion, which have sustained the spiritual life and faith of the believers. Pope Pius XII defended the validity of pious exercises in his encyclical *Mediator Dei* (1947), which are now regarded as Catholic piety. In the Constitution, *Sacrosanctum Concilium*, Vatican II reaffirmed the primacy of the Liturgy and the validity of popular piety.

This lack of respect for popular piety, according to the *Directory*, is the result of "an inadequate understanding of certain ecclesial realities and is not infrequently the product not so much of the doctrine of the faith, but of some ideologically inspired prejudice." In some cases, the critics of popular devotion refuse to recognize the power of the Holy Spirit present in these pious exercises. In their quest for the so-called "pure Liturgy," the idealists also fail to recognize the fruits that popular devotions can produce. Not being in touch with historical reality, they mistakenly label popular piety as distorted "sentimentality."[5]

On the other hand, the *Directory* also acknowledges that too much free-hand practice of popular piety can be harmful to the Liturgy. This happens when a particular popular devotion becomes a substitute for Church worship: "it becomes a cultic expression extraneous to the comprehension and sensibility of the people which is destined to be neglected, relegated to a secondary role or even become reserved to particular groups."[6]

Thus, the *Directory* warns against an over-emphasis on the importance of popular devotions because such a one-sided exaltation fails to take into account the fact that "the essential elements of the Liturgy derive from the will of Christ himself, and is unable to emphasize its indispensable soteriological and doxological importance."[7] The church believes that

---

4. *Directory on Popular Piety and the Liturgy*, no. 46.
5. Ibid., no. 50.
6. Ibid., no. 51.
7. Ibid., no. 55.

the perfect worship of God comes only through the Liturgy, namely the Eucharist, which celebrates the passion, death, resurrection, and ascension of Christ, and the coming of the Holy Spirit. This belief, however, does not exclude the importance and validity of other pious exercises.

The Church is concerned that a disregard for the importance of the Liturgy might lead to a distorted understanding of the Christian mystery regarding the saving action of Jesus Christ and the work of the Holy Spirit. It also leads to a failure to appreciate the importance of salvation history, and the relationship between the Old and the New Testaments. Hence, exaggeration of the importance of popular piety would underrate the Word of God that sustains the Liturgy and would eventually lead to "a loss of the *sensus Ecclesiae*."[8] This means the failure to think along with the Church and to maintain unity with the rest of the faithful in the world. The *Directory* is strongly opposed to an exclusive promotion of certain popular devotion that relies solely on cosmic, natural religions and other forms of cultural or ethical expressions—all of which lead the faithful away from Christian revelation.

While warning against excessiveness of popular piety, the *Directory* acknowledges it as a legitimate expression of Christian spirituality. Popular devotion can provide the Liturgy with insights into inculturation and accommodation because of its creativity and dynamism. A fruitful and harmonious relationship of Liturgy and popular piety must be maintained. This is because participation in the Eucharist alone is not enough for a believer's spiritual life to grow if he/she is lacking in personal prayer.

Possessing an innate sense of the sacred, popular piety reveals a longing for God, his love, and his mercy. It promotes an interior disposition of patience, and the ability to bear sufferings. When channeled carefully, popular devotions can lead the faithful into the mystery of Christ's suffering, death, and resurrection. Popular piety also encourages contemplation of the afterlife, the communion of saints, the Blessed Virgin Mary, the angels, and prayers for the faithful departed. The *Directory* states: "In genuine forms of popular piety, the Gospel message assimilates expressive forms particular to a given culture while also permeating the consciousness of that culture with the content of the Gospel, and its idea of life and death, and of man's freedom, mission and destiny."[9]

---

8. Ibid., no, 56.
9. Ibid., no. 63.

Thus, both the gospel and the culture of a specific place enrich each other. The Church acknowledges the importance of popular piety in preserving the faith of the people, and as a method of evangelization. This is especially important in areas where there is a lack of pastoral care and evangelization effort. In such a situation, the faithful express their faith through popular piety, which is a "starting point in deepening the faith of the people and in bringing it to maturity."[10]

The Church's main concern is that some popular devotions may lack sufficient Christian elements such as the death and resurrection of Christ, the importance of belonging to the church, and the action of the Holy Spirit in the lives of the faithful. Lack of direct contact with sacred Scriptures and isolation from the sacraments of the church are also another possible deviation of popular piety. There is also a tendency to see popular devotion as purely utilitarian, without commitment to gospel values. In spite of some deficiencies, the Church acknowledges that popular piety bears Trinitarian signs. It promotes a sense of God's goodness and mercy, his power and wisdom, and especially his love for the poor and lowly.

Who touched my clothes?

> And a woman was there who had been subject to bleeding for twelve years. When she heard about Jesus, she came up behind him in the crowd and touched his cloak, because she thought, "If I just touch his clothes, I will be healed." Immediately her bleeding stopped and she felt in her body that she was freed from her suffering.
>
> At once Jesus realized that power had gone out from him. He turned around in the crowd and asked, "Who touched my clothes?" "You see the people crowding against you," his disciples answered, "and yet you can ask, 'Who touched me?'" But Jesus kept looking around to see who had done it.
>
> Then the woman, knowing what had happened to her, came and fell at his feet and, trembling with fear, told him the whole truth. He said to her, "Daughter, your faith has healed you. Go in peace and be freed from your suffering." (Matt 9:20–22.)

In this incident, which was reported by all three evangelists, the sick woman held onto one utterly simple belief in mind—that by touching an object associated with Christ, such as the hem of his garment, she would

---

10. Ibid., no. 64.

experience the same power of healing as if she had made a direct plea to the Lord.

This is perhaps one of the most dramatic examples of popular piety—the single belief that God's grace and power will still work and be channeled to ordinary people through one simple pious act regardless of the individual's lack of knowledge or understanding of church doctrine or liturgy. Nonetheless, when the miracle has taken place, the Lord *does* require that the supplicant acknowledges openly the act of divine grace. God does not want anyone to get a secret free pass, so to speak.

Back to the present day, the *Directory* requires that we maintain a balance between liturgy and popular piety so that there is a sense of direction. The operating word here is harmony—maintaining a harmonious relationship between the official worship of the Church in the liturgy and the practice of popular devotion. The *Directory* provides a sense of direction to pastoral work by its emphasis on the central role of the paschal mystery—the suffering, death, and resurrection of Christ—in our Christian faith. This means all practices of popular piety must be oriented towards this mystery—this is the "common denominator" that transcends time and space, which has influenced the manner and form of worship at any given time in history.[11]

For human beings, comprised of mind, body, and heart, popular piety caters to our need to express the paschal mystery in a manner that is meaningful and relevant to our culture and time. Without proper direction, there is danger that our acts of devotion may turn inward towards the human and cosmic rather than towards the mystery of our redemption. The *Directory* thus provides a set of guidelines to be followed prudently rather than a set of laws to be implemented dogmatically.

Sacramentals

On the danger that our devotions may be self-serving, turning inward towards the human and cosmic, rather than towards the paschal mystery, we need to understand that we cannot force God to grant us favors. If we think that sacramentals can be used to persuade God to grant our wishes, we are verging on superstition in our attempt to manipulate him. This was a significant problem in the Middle Ages, when the Church was selling indulgences. Our relationship with God should be based on love and not on

---

11. Abeyasingha, "Popular piety and liturgy," 22.

bargaining. God grants us our prayers according to his will, not according to our manipulation. Nonetheless, sacramentals such as holy objects or actions can strengthen our devotion and make us more receptive to his grace. In other words, "sacramentals work on the *receiving* end and sacraments work on the *giving* end."[12]

Sacramentals such as the rosary, icon, scapular, and the gesture of making the sign of the cross serve as a reminder that we rely on the power of God; these objects and simple acts encourage us to pray consistently. We are immediately brought to the presence of God at the sight of the crucifix on the wall or the statue of the Blessed Virgin Mary. *The Catechism of the Catholic Church* states: "Sacramentals do not confer the grace of the Holy Spirit in the way that the sacraments do, but by the Church's prayer, they prepare us to receive grace and dispose us to cooperate with it."[13] Any proper use of material things can be directed towards the praise of God. Like sacraments, sacramentals draw their power from the passion, death, and resurrection of Christ.

The *Directory* reminds us that we should avoid the extreme of over-spiritualization on the one hand, and on the other hand, the complete disregard of sacramentals as part of our Christian living. As humans, we are dependent on sights, sounds, smell, and touch to communicate with one another as well as with God. Sacramentals serve as a means to experience divine reality. Nonetheless, there is a school of thought in the Church that discourages popular piety, which gave impetus to the Protestant Reformation in the sixteenth century. Most famous among the advocates of this spirituality is Desiderius Erasmus (1466–1536), a Dutch humanist scholar and Catholic priest.

Erasmus of Rotterdam

Concerned primarily with understanding the Scriptures and being critical of religion that fixed itself upon ritual and ceremony and regarded them as piety, Erasmus also criticized people who worshipped saints with certain rites and rightly insisted that worship must be directed to Christ. Veneration of saints must be detached from any consideration of material benefits or creature comforts. Erasmus considered the worship of saints as a kind of superstition. His criticism also included those who pray for a long life, good

---

12. Zyromski, "Sacramentals," 27.
13. *Catechism of the Catholic Church*, no. 1670.

health, and riches only for their own sake. This kind of piety is actually an "impiety," according to Erasmus.[14] For him, perfect piety means moving from the visible to the invisible; this is the only way to a purer, spiritual life. In concrete terms, we must reject the visible world for the world unseen.

Sympathetic toward the uneducated who practiced a kind of "ingenuous superstition," Erasmus attacked mainly those people who portrayed themselves as devout by encouraging the ignorance of the common people.[15] Perhaps he was attacking the priests and monks during this time for promoting the superstitious beliefs among simple people for the priests' own material gains. In other words, self-serving Church leaders encouraged some kind of superstitions for their own benefits such as the selling of indulgences and relics.

Critical of people worshipping Christ in visible ceremonies for the sake of material benefits, Erasmus believed that possessing this kind of self-serving mentality, they became "diverted *from* Christ by those very practices."[16] He wrote: "I am ashamed to report how gullibly most of those people look upon certain mere ceremonies, invented by little men . . . how odiously they press these ceremonies upon others, how confidently they rely upon them, how boldly they judge other men, how belligerently they eye them."[17]

Erasmus was referring to those who hold the office of censor in the church whom he believed to be "sodden with certain melancholy vices," worse than pagans who at least possessed certain common virtues instilled by natural reason and experience. The censors, very obviously, are worse than the pagans because they are "unteachable, intractable, quarrelsome, greedy for sensual pleasures but queasy at the Word of God, agreeable to no one, evilly suspicious of everyone else but indulgent of themselves."[18] The practice of the spiritual life, according to Erasmus, consists in loving one another rather than taking part in rituals. In other words, we need to help the oppressed, defend the orphans, and protect the widows. He is not demanding that we should neglect the teachings and traditions of the Church, but that we should move from the visible forms of worship, such as statues, to the worship of God in spirit.

14. Erasmus, *The Enchiridion of Erasmus*, 100.
15. Ibid.
16. Ibid., 114.
17. Ibid., 115.
18. Ibid., 115–16.

Be that as it may, Erasmus acknowledged that ingenuous superstition in the poor and simple-minded people might have positive effects. In fact, superstitious beliefs can be developed into genuine faith through proper catechizing. John Henry Newman was one of those who held this conviction and maintained that superstition in simple people might be better than the skepticism of the educated.

Companion of faith

In the Preface to the third edition of his *Via Media*, John Henry Newman (1801–1890) mentions a certain bishop who sanctions public veneration of dubious relics and who tolerates such popular devotion because it helps the people towards true worship. The bishop does not guarantee the truth of these relics but he approves and praises the piety of the people, which was not very well founded. Newman seems to suggest that a little superstitious belief may do no harm but may help awaken true faith. He calls for tolerance because rooting out the error may do more harm than good:

> Such may be the feeling under which the Church takes part in popular religious manifestations without subjecting them to theological and historical criticism; she is in a choice of difficulties; did she act otherwise, she would be rooting up the wheat with the intruding weeds; she would be "quenching the smoking flax," and endangering the faith and loyalty of a city or a district, for the sake of an intellectual precision which was quite out of place and was not asked of her.[19]

In other words, Church leaders have the duty to condemn pious frauds but they must be aware that errors of fact may do no harm while their removal may have a widespread negative impact on the faithful. Referring to the woman who touched the garment of Jesus, Newman maintains that "as to the mere countenancing of superstitions, it must not be forgotten, that our Lord Himself, on one occasion passed over the superstitious act of a woman who was in great trouble, for the merit of the faith which was the real element in it."[20]

Under the influence of superstitious belief, she was rewarded with a miracle. In fact, she "paid a sort of fetish reverence" to the hem of Jesus'

---

19. Newman, *Via Media*, 16:lxvi.
20. Ibid., 17:lxviii

garment and was hoping that "virtue would go out of him, without his knowing it."[21] Jesus does not regard the woman's faith as an "idolatrous act ... for in His new law He was opening the meaning of the word 'idolatry,' and applying it to various sins, to the adulation paid to rich men, to the thirst after material gain, to ambition, and the pride of life, idolatries worse in His judgment than the idolatry of ignorance, but not commonly startling or shocking to educated minds."[22]

While Jesus insists on the necessity of faith, he is silent regarding the danger of superstition. Perhaps we can see superstition as related to earnest faith, a weakness prevalent among simple people that can be conceded. Newman considers it as the "sure companion of faith," a price we pay for our enthusiasm in the faith.[23] It also reminds us of the importance of the sacramental system in our Catholic belief. While it is important that the priestly office in the Church maintains vigilance regarding the purity of faith, the Church must also allow the prophetic voice of her people to be heard. The line between true faith and superstition can be difficult to discern at times. Further, there is always a tendency for religious belief to be blended with superstition that arises from a particular culture. It needs not be regarded as corruption, but rather the ability of the faith to blend into the native culture. Traces of such belief in a religion are a sign that it has been inculturated and accommodated in a particular society. There is no such thing as pure Christianity, as some Christians would like us to believe.

Newman feared more the danger of unbelief than that of superstition: "I will not shrink from uttering my firm conviction, that it would be a gain to this country, were it vastly more superstitious, more bigoted, more gloomy, more fierce in its religion, than at present it shows itself to be."[24] Due to the weakness of human nature, Newman believed a little superstition could actually be the beginning of true faith. Of course, he admitted that the Church must be vigilant so that the faith would not be degraded, but stated that considering the present state of unbelief in England and the world at large, superstition may not be the worst of evils. At any rate, Newman was inclined "to doubt whether that nation really had the faith, which is free in all its ranks and classes from all kinds and degrees of what

---

21. Ibid.
22. Ibid., no. 18:lxix
23. Ibid.
24. Newman, "The Religion of the Day," 2:320.

is commonly considered superstition."[25] He was convinced that to be contemptuous of superstition is to be contemptuous of religion as such.[26]

Newman even went to the extent of regarding superstition as "man's truest and best religion, *before* the Gospel shines on him." And thus, "to be superstitious—is nature's best offering, her most acceptable service, her most mature and enlarged wisdom, in the presence of a holy and offended God. They who are not superstitious without the Gospel, will not be religious with it: and I would that even in us, who have the Gospel, there were more of superstition than there is."[27] The fear of God is the beginning of wisdom and so is a little superstition. He writes:

> This is the idolatry of a refined age, in which the superstitions of barbarous times displease, in consequence of their grossness. Men congratulate themselves on their emancipation from forms and their enlightened worship, when they are but in the straight course to a worse captivity, and are exchanging dependence on the creature for dependence on self.[28]

Newman was more sympathetic towards the offerings of primitive people than the intellectuals of his time, who were skeptics, influenced by the philosophies of Epicureans and Pelagians. He accepted the idea that superstition can play a role in leading an individual towards the true faith.

The success of the early church, with its Jewish roots, was due to its willingness to enter into the cultural life of the Roman-Hellenistic world. "Without sacrificing doctrinal purity she preserved from the old culture whatever was good, transformed whatever was indifferent, and with a view to gradual catharsis from within tolerated much that was considered evil, but not intrinsically or irremediably so."[29] In other words, the church accommodated the culture of the pagan world, retained what was good, and tolerated what was considered evil, such as superstition, with a view of purging it eventually.

This brings us to the Chinese cult of ancestor veneration, which posed a challenge to the Catholic practice of popular piety towards the dead as demonstrated by the so-called Rites Controversy during the seventeenth and eighteenth centuries.

25. Newman, *Via Media*, 18:lxx.
26. Short, "John Henry Newman in the 'realms of superstition,'" 68.
27. Newman, "On Justice, as a Principle of Divine Governance," 4:118–19.
28. Newman, *Lectures on the Doctrine of Justification*, 4:324.
29. Dunne, *Generation of Giants*, 6.

Rites Controversy

Honoring the memory of one's ancestors occupies a significant part in popular piety in many cultures in Africa and Asia. The desire to prolong family and social links with one's dead relatives, particularly those who had gained high office or valor, is an integral part of the human nature. Influenced by cultural and religious elements with its own anthropological concepts, this practice or cult of venerating the dead is well established, and still widely practiced in many contemporary cultures.

The *Directory* suggests great caution when evaluating such customs to make sure they are not contrary to gospel values. At the same time, we must also not be too hasty to dismiss the customs as pagan practices. This was the painful lesson the Church learned from the Rites Controversy that took place in China during the seventeenth and eighteenth centuries. Theologically challenging, this particular historical episode demonstrates the importance of inculturation in popular piety towards the dead.

Influenced by local religious folklore and Confucian principles of parental obedience, the cult of ancestor veneration has been an important social and political aspect of the Chinese way of life. Thus, the failure to accommodate and accept this practice became a stumbling block for evangelization of China as well as among the Chinese Diaspora. It is timely that the *Directory* reminds us of the need for pastoral prudence in addressing the relationship between Liturgy and popular piety practices and insists that there must be harmony between worship and veneration. Christian principles must form the basis of popular piety, which means placing emphasis on the Paschal Mystery, the immortality of the soul, and the communion of saints. The church teaches not only that prayers for the dead are capable of helping them but also that the intercession of the dead is also effective in helping us.

Sacred and Profane

The Rites Controversy seen from a Western perspective was a matter of determining if the practice was religious and thus presumably superstitious, or civil, and thus non-superstitious. The rites were condemned because they were deemed superstitious. However, the word *superstitious* is fraught with ambiguity. We tend to dismiss other religious beliefs as superstitious when they come into conflict with our own creed or when they are contrary to what we hold as true. We tend to be pre-judgmental. It is important to note that superstition covers a wide spectrum of meanings, from idolatry to magic. In the Christian context, superstition refers to a violation of the first commandment: "I am the Lord your God, who brought you out of the land of Egypt, out of the house of slavery; you shall have no other gods before me" (Exod 20: 2–3).

Regarding ancestor veneration, the Chinese word *Ji* (祭) literally means festive occasion. It can also mean to offer sacrifice, to worship, or to remember and pay respect to the deceased. Some Western missionaries regarded ancestor veneration merely as *ji si* (祭祀), worship, which led to a lot of misunderstanding. In fact, they regarded paying respect to the dead in the Chinese context as ancestor worship. As we shall see, the situation is rather complex, with the weak understanding of the tradition/custom, resulting in the so-called "Rites Controversy."

In the East, the sacred-profane dichotomy is rarely visible: the religious world and the secular world are fused together in various cultic and cultural expressions. Confucian and ancestor veneration rites are the means to hold the community together through appropriate rituals, which are drawn from both the sacred and profane spheres. In the West, the religious and the secular are kept as distinct, but in the East, they coalesce in the ritual act.[30]

As mentioned earlier, Newman remarks that to be contemptuous of superstition is to be contemptuous of religion. Those who are not superstitious without the gospel will not be religious with it. The sacred and profane are not two distinct, separate spheres; they often merge in our civil and religious ceremonies. The cult of ancestor veneration serves to maintain good order and harmony in Chinese society besides promoting filial piety. The Rites Controversy is about the proper connection between ties of kinship, community, and God, which popular piety can help to enhance. Thus, ancestor veneration embedded in Chinese culture could be carefully and prudently incorporated into Christian popular piety, such as in observing All Souls' Day and offering suffrage for the souls in purgatory with an emphasis on the immortality of the souls and the communion of saints.

---

30. Luttio, "The Chinese Rites Controversy (1603–1742)," 312–13.

Superstition and Piety

Two Traditions

Veneration of ancestors in the Confucian tradition recorded in the *Analects* has to do with handling parents' funeral arrangements, mourning, and performing the appropriate rites. The purpose is to improve the moral standard of society. Remembrance of one's ancestors is only a cultural expression, not a religious one. However among the simple people in the Chinese diaspora, ancestor worship is a core element of folk religions. Fr. Simon Wong, a Hong Kong Jesuit, testifies:

> Born and bred in Hong Kong, a place with the Chinese culture as the core, however, my personal experiences of ancestor remembrance differ significantly from the idea of the *Analects*. Ever since I was a small boy, I have been hearing my mother praying to our ancestors during the Chinese New Year and at other festivals. From what my mother was praying, it was very obvious that she saw ancestors as transcendent spirits who were able to bless and protect her family. This is no single incident but is a core element in the folk religions in the Chinese-speaking world. I can testify from my personal experiences that ancestor remembrance carries religious connotations.[31]

Confucius's teaching regarding remembering and paying respect to ancestors relates merely to a civil ceremony devoid of any religious significance. However, when it is practiced at the grassroots level, especially among the simple people in the villages, it turns out to be a pious practice, a spiritual exercise of ancestor worship. This was what the Dominican friars witnessed in the villages in Fukien Province in China in the sixteenth century. The Rites Controversy led to the church's promulgation of the following decrees.

Pope Innocent X

Decree of the Sacred Congregation for the Propagation of the Faith, September 12, 1645. This document, approved by Pope Innocent X, was the first judgment by Rome on the Rites Controversy. Rome condemned the Jesuits for allowing Chinese Christians to take part in local rites for the veneration of ancestors. The decree forbids Christians to take part in sacrifices offered at Confucius's temple nor are they allowed to assist at sacrifices honoring

---

31. Wong, "A Dogmatic and Liturgical Examination of Ancestor Remembrance."

ancestors. To preserve the memory of their ancestors, the Chinese use tablets with the names of the deceased written on them. They believe that the souls of the dead are present in the tablets to receive sacrifices and offerings. In this document, the Church forbids Christians to keep these tablets in their homes.[32]

Pope Clement XI

Apostolic Constitution, *Ex illa die*, by Pope Clement XI, March 19, 1715, as found in *Ex quo singulari* of Benedict XIV, July 11, 1742. Here the pope prescribes an oath to be taken by missionaries who are or will be missionaries in China. Obviously there were missionaries, especially members of the Society of Jesus, who did not follow the decrees regarding Chinese rites or ceremonies. This *Apostolic Constitution* decrees that Christians should not be permitted to serve or to be present at the solemn sacrifices, which Chinese make to Confucius and their ancestors. These ceremonies are considered to be tainted with superstition. Christians are also not allowed to offer oblation to their ancestors in temples or shrines dedicated to them, in private homes and tombs.[33]

Pope Pius XII

Plane compertum est, December 8, 1939, approved by Pope Pius XII. This instruction *of Propaganda Fide* brought the Chinese Rites Controversy to an official end. After years of reflection and debate, the church finally realized that the honors paid to Confucius are not religious in themselves, but rather civil honors. Therefore, Christians can participate in them. It is also lawful and proper that Christians remember and pay respect toward the deceased just as Catholics do on All Souls' Day. Hence, all clergy are dispensed from the obligation of taking the *Ex quo singulari* oath.[34]

The Church now recognizes that some ceremonies in Asia, although in earlier times they were connected with pagan rites, are now merely civil expressions of filial piety, nationalism, or patriotism. Chinese Catholics are now allowed to be present at testimonials honoring Confucius and to hold

---

32. Hunt, *The Gospel among the Nations*, 73–75.
33. Ibid., 76–77.
34. Ibid., 80.

tablets in honor of Confucius in buildings or schools dedicated to him. Bowing of heads and other acts of civil honor before the deceased or the image of the deceased is now permissible.[35]

As you can see, we have come a long way—what was regarded as superstitious is now seen as expression of cultural beliefs. The Rites Controversy, started during the seventeenth and eighteenth centuries, officially ended only in 1939. It was more a misunderstanding among Europeans regarding Chinese religious and cultural practices. For the faithful Catholic Chinese, it was a long and painful wait. Lamentably, no Chinese clerics or theologians were consulted on this important issue.

An examination of popular religion, in this case ancestor veneration in China, tells us much about how people practice their religious beliefs within their own cultural context. Religious practices and beliefs are never as clear-cut and precise as we like to think. As mentioned earlier, there is much ambiguity regarding the practice of popular piety, which I think is normal and understandable. Our motivations are usually mixed—we may profess the same faith with different motivations and we may draw different conclusions about what faith means to each one of us.

Catholic Church in Hong Kong

The Catholic Church in Hong Kong has given space to the laity in the liturgy to remember their ancestors. However, it has been made clear to the faithful that their ancestors are not deities and thus cannot be worshipped. Therefore, when we adopt some traditional practice of using flowers or food in the liturgy, these are not meant to be "offerings" to the ancestors, but mere expressions of love, thanksgiving, and respect. It is the custom of Chinese to bring fruits and other kinds of gifts when visiting friends and families. The same principle applies to ancestor veneration: "All material things we use in ancestor remembrance are but secondary symbols signifying our love and fond memories of our ancestors. It is critically important not to take presents as 'offerings' to ancestors, as this is superstitious and hence heretical."[36]

The Lunar New Year, an important Chinese festival, has an influence on Catholic liturgy in Hong Kong. Besides the liturgies for Sunday, Easter, and Christmas, there are also special masses for the Lunar New Year, Ching

35. Ibid., 80–81.
36. Ibid.

Ming Festival, and Chung Yeung Festival. If the Lunar New Year day falls on the same day as Ash Wednesday, fasting and abstinence are dispensed and postponed to another day. On this festive occasion, parishes are decorated, mandarin oranges symbolizing prosperity are distributed, and red packets (*lai see*) with money are given to priests, friends, and loved ones. The parishes too offer *lai see* to the congregation and special blessings are given for the occasion.

Like All Souls' Day, Ching Ming and Chung Yeung are festivals where Chinese families gather together to pay respect to their ancestors. In the past, during Chung Yeung Festival, people climbed mountains to avoid bad luck. Gradually, they began to visit the graves to pay respect to their ancestors. Eventually, the social and cultural meaning of these two festivals merged.[37] The Catholic Church responds positively to these two festivals with requiem masses organized on both occasions.

Some Catholics continue to offer incense, to burn joss sticks, to their ancestors to express their respect and love for the deceased. They perform this so-called pagan exercise to avoid conflict; they want to maintain peace, harmony, and unity within the family especially when their parents are non-Catholics. They do this without contradicting their own Christian principles, but for the love of their families. This is very much in line with Vatican II's call for reconciliation and accommodation. Some Catholics continue to keep the old traditional rituals or other practices that carry cosmologies and value-orientations originated from Buddhism, Taoism, or Chinese popular religions. They do not want to be cut off from family history and tradition. In view of this, the Church can raise cultural awareness among Catholics so as to facilitate discussion and reflection in order to minimize frictions among family members with disparity of cult.

---

37. Li, Cheung, and Chan, "Hong Kong," 224.

Chapter 6

Our Lady of Medjugorje

Since 2004, Rev. Peter Leung Tat-choy, a diocesan priest in Hong Kong, has been leading groups of Chinese pilgrims from Toronto and Hong Kong to Medjugorje. He has witnessed numerous conversions, broken families reunited, and profound changes in the faith of the people who journeyed with him. When I asked him what initially motivated him to lead the pilgrims to this small mountain village in Eastern Europe, he merely replied, "People asked me, that is all." In other words, he was needed and he responded to their request. Now Fr. Leung is convinced of the importance of the message of Medjugorje, which includes fasting on Wednesdays and Fridays, a regime which he follows faithfully.

Medjugorje, a small mountain village in Eastern Europe, has become the center of a global movement that promotes solidarity, forgiveness, and reconciliation. Advances in communication and transportation, and the availability of cheaper air travel, have enabled thousands of pilgrims from all parts of the globe to visit Medjugorje, where many experience peace and consolation.

This chapter discusses the historical background of Marian devotion with a focus on the apparitions in Medjugorje. The events that occurred in this secluded mountain village in the Bosnia-Hercegovina region have now achieved global significance. The two personal testimonies I have included here are of pilgrims from Canada and China (Hong Kong). This chapter maintains that the message of peace proclaimed by the Virgin Mary at Medjugorje and her call for conversion is more urgent than ever in our world plagued by political, cultural, and religious conflicts. Torn as we are by rivalries and disillusioned by rampant materialism, the message of the Queen of Peace gives us hope that another world is not only possible but also necessary. Medjugorje matters because its message is ecumenical and universal.

Started in 1981, the Marian apparitions at Medjugorje have attracted a lot of attention internationally. In fact, the numbers of pilgrims going to Medjugorje compare favorably to those visiting the shrines at Fatima and Lourdes. However, Medjugorje apparitions cannot be simply viewed as just another visionary event because there are certain characteristics that attract special notice from critics. Shrouded in controversies, the visions occurred in a politically and culturally volatile region. There were rumors that the site of apparitions reveals the Madonna's support for Croats' nationalistic aspirations. In addition, there were intra-ecclesiastical conflicts between the Franciscan friars who have been in the region since the fourteenth century, and the diocesan clergy who attempted to take over their parishes in recent times.

Critics believe the alleged apparitions have transformed Medjugorje into a movement with ethnic-political and intra-ecclesiastical ramifications. Sabrina Ramet speaks of the "manifest functions" of Medjugorje such as the healing of the sick through divine intervention, and the "latent functions" such as promoting solidarity among Catholic Croats. In addition, the apparitions at Medjugorje may also serve as a "concealed function" of reinforcing the members of the Franciscan Order in their dispute with the diocesan clergy.[1] What is striking is that Medjugorje provokes strong reactions from both sides: support from the pilgrims that flock there by the thousands, and strong opposition from the diocesan clergy against the Franciscans who promote it. In fact, the local bishop attempted to suppress it altogether.

Be that as it may, devotion to the Medjugorje Madonna and apparitions continues, crossing confessional and national boundaries. Catholic Centers dedicated to Our Lady of Medjugorje have been established all over the world, attracting even Protestants and Muslims. Distinguished theologians such as Robert Faricy, Hans Urs Von Balthasar, and René Laurentin spoke favorably of the movement. John Paul II was reported to have

---

1. Ramet, "The miracle at Medjugorje," 170. Some material in this chapter appeared in Mong, "Medjugorje Matters," 1/129–9/137; 14/142.

said: "If I were not the Pope, I would probably [have] visited Medjugorje by now."[2]

Marian Apparitions

Apparition can be defined as a "specific kind of vision in which a person or being not normally within the visionary's perceptual range appears to that person, not in a world apart as in a dream, and not as a modification of a concrete object as in the case of a weeping icon or moving statue, but as a part of the environment, without apparent connection to verifiable visual stimuli."[3] Once validated, apparitions provide clarity on what the divine will is at a specific time.[4]

During the last 200 years many devout Catholics have visited rural areas in various parts of the world where the Virgin Mary is alleged to have appeared to some people, usually children or young people. Some people visit these places out of curiosity but the majority journey in faith, hoping to be granted special graces from the Blessed Virgin herself. To experience the apparition of the Madonna is a privilege granted to very few people. However, many pilgrims have experienced profound conversion, which instills a deep impact in their lives.

Marian apparitions have always attracted attention from both detractors and devotees. Stories that emanate from some believers who have visited Marian shrines describe extraordinary visions that appear in specific places such as Lourdes, Fatima, and La Salette. The majority of the people tell of less dramatic experiences such as the unusual appearance of the sun, while others witness the Virgin's strong presence and intervention such as the healing of people who are sick, physically, emotionally, and spiritually. It is always about the Virgin's presence and about asking for her intervention to offer healing to afflicted people in our troubled word. In most of these Marian apparitions, we witness the transformation of private experience into public belief, the transformation of the suffering of a particular people and the suffering of the world. This transformation is often accompanied by a sense of crisis, which is apocalyptic.[5]

---

2. Wiinikka-Lydon, "The ambivalence of Medjugorje," 2.
3. Zimdars-Swartz, *Encountering Mary*, 4.
4. See Malina, "From Isis to Medjugorje," 79–80.
5. Zimdars-Swartz, *Encountering Mary*, xiv.

Power of Popular Piety

Marian devotion began to flourish during the eleventh and twelfth centuries in Europe. The Virgin Mary has always been the prime figure in Christian apparitions. During the Reformation, the appearance of the Virgin seemed greatly reduced. But it was revived during the nineteenth and twentieth centuries with reports focused on some sites where the Virgin was reported to have appeared. According to Zimdars-Swartz, these "modern Marian apparitions have become focal points for what appears to be a significant revival of interest in the supernatural in many parts of the Christian world."[6]

Modern Marian apparition has its roots in Marian piety and devotion in the Middle Ages, which emphasized the Virgin's intercessory power to help those who are in need. Between the eleventh and twelfth centuries, devotion to saints had grown around particular tombs or relics, such as the shrine of Thomas Beckett, Archbishop of Canterbury, a martyr. Eventually, this devotion gave way to devotion to the Virgin who was believed more powerful to protect and assist people who were in trouble.

Mary's appearance in the early Middle Ages usually led to "shrine-establishment apparitions," which suggested some kind of ecclesiastical approval to local Marian piety.[7] Some of these sites have developed into enormous shrines proclaiming a universal message to the world. Initially, it was believed that Mary appeared to members of a community that was suffering or whose existence was being threatened and the Virgin suggested a solution usually in the form of prayers and penance.

Most of the witnesses of extraordinary visions in the early years of Christianity were by monks, nuns, priests, and members of religious orders, who were known for their piety. They were sought by the faithful for their ability to heal, read consciences, and give advice to popes and kings. Later in the Middle Ages, men and women who were not members of religious orders claimed to have seen visions. Most of the seers in the modern ages took over this role and were expected to conform to this kind of late medieval visionary. Present day visionaries or seers are normal people with no exceptional talent or holiness but are given the gift of prophecy and extraordinary power during the time of the apparition. Some have entered religious life after witnessing the apparitions.[8]

---

6. Ibid., 5.
7. Ibid., 8.
8. Ibid., 9.

In the treatise *De servorum Dei beatificatione*, by Pope Benedict XIV (1740–1758), the Catholic Church gave an official approval to private apparitions, after careful investigation to make public the revelation "for the instruction and good of the faithful." However, this should not be considered the assent of Catholic faith (*fides catholica*) but the assent of human faith (*fides humana*) made with prudence. Thus one can refuse assent to those revelations with good reasons.[9] In fact, Pope Emeritus Benedict XVI taught that the Church never requires the faithful to believe in apparitions, not even those recognized by the Church.

The bishop in whose diocese the apparition is said to have occurred has the right to decide if the vision is worthy of "the assent of human faith." The diocesan commission's negative decision, that the apparition is not worthy of human faith, can work both ways: it can discourage pilgrims, such as in the case at Fehrbach (Kreis Pirmasens) in Germany, and it can also give impetus to the devotion as happened with the apparitions at Garabandal, Spain, and also at San Damiano, Italy, in the 1960s. As we shall see, the bishop's disapproval of the apparitions at Medjugorje encouraged more fervent devotion. To accept an apparition means to recognize its divine origin; to reject an apparition means to claim that it is just a natural occurrence. This is essentially a judgment of faith and not an empirical judgment in the final analysis.[10] Such is the teaching of the Church regarding apparitions as stated in *De servorum Dei beatificatione* of Pope Benedict XIV.

While the powers of saints have been less and less emphasized, the powers and special privileges of Mary have been emphasized more and more since the early Middle Ages. This emphasis of the Virgin's ascendancy culminated in the official proclamation of Mary's bodily assumption into heaven by Pope Pius XII at the close of the Marian year in 1950. This proclamation obviously has a great impact on the interest in Marian apparitions: "the belief that one can obtain special privileges or graces through devotional exercises which express or help to establish a special relationship with the Virgin Mary."[11] Medjugorje, like the other popular Marian shrines such as Lourdes and Fatima, is a fine example of such expressions of piety taking place. However, as we shall see, Medjugorje has some striking differences that make it controversial and intriguing for scholars and critics.

---

9. Ibid.
10. Ibid., 10–11.
11. Ibid., 10.

Viper Region

The mountain terrain of southern Hercegovina where Medjugorje is located is called "viper region" in reference to the abundance of poisonous snakes there, and also to the Herzegovinian temperament.[12] It is a region that has bred violent nationalists, bandits, and war criminals. Critics and opponents thus find the idea of Medjugorje being transformed into an oasis of peace and holiness both incredulous and ludicrous. But the fact is that since June 1981, millions of Christians and non-Christians from all over the world have visited Medjugorje because six children from ages ten to seventeen in 1981 were alleged to have seen apparitions of the Virgin Mary, who is known in the region as *Gospa* (Madonna).

Skeptics believe that Catholic nations experiencing crisis and anxiety are liable to have this kind of vision. Opposing the alleged apparitions at Medjugorje, the Bishop of Mostar, Ratko Perić, believes they were based on "some childish stories and hallucinations." In 1995, following the official position of the church, Perić asserted that the Medjugorje parish church has not been declared a Marian shrine and "no cult of the Madonna based upon so-called apparitions has ever been proclaimed."[13]

The Yugoslav Bishops' Commission issued "The Declaration of Zadar," which constitutes the official position of the Catholic Church regarding the apparitions at Medjugorje (Congregation for the Doctrine and Faith, March 23, 1996, protocol 154/81–01985). The commission concludes that the supernatural character of the visions in Medjugorje "cannot be established."[14] Thus no official pilgrimages to Medjugorje are permitted, and Medjugorje is not an officially approved Marian Shrine. Supporters of Medjugorje insist that this declaration does not constitute the final words of the Church regarding the divine nature of the apparitions.

Former Archbishop of Spilt, France Franic, supported the Medjugorje movement. In 1987, he clarified that the Church's prohibition of pilgrimages to Medjugorje as a place of Marian apparitions only referred to those organized by the bishops. It does not refer to private pilgrimages organized by individuals and those led by priests or religious. Thus pilgrims from around the world continue to flock to Medjugorje because they understand these apparitions as revelations of God through the Virgin at various sites

12. Herrero, "Medjugorje," 139.
13. Ibid., 140.
14. Ibid., 146.

throughout the world. The messages given by the Virgin are apocalyptic in nature, telling of the end times or "the last days." They speak of the battle between good and evil, and the Madonna protecting her children under her tender care.

Franciscan Foundation

From the fourteenth century to the beginning of 1960, the Franciscan Order (OFM) had been the main evangelization force in the Diocese of Mostar, which includes the parish of Medjugorje. During the 400 years of Turkish domination, Franciscan friars remained the only ecclesiastical presence in Bosnia-Hercegovina. Many of them suffered persecution and martyrdom at the hands of Ottoman leaders. In spite of this threat, the friars were able to reach some kind of agreement with the relatively tolerant Muslims rulers. They were also successful in fighting against the Bogomil heresy, which plagued the church in Bosnia during the Turkish occupation.[15] Such diligence, devotion, and dedication endeared the Franciscans to the Bosnian Croats who regarded the friars as their spiritual leaders: "the people of Bosnia and Hercegovina consider the Franciscans to be living cell of their own bodies. The Franciscans share the people's joys and sorrows, and the people call them their 'uncles.'"[16]

The original intention of the Franciscan missionaries was to set up a diocesan structure, which would eventually hand over to the secular clergy. This was what Rome understood anyway.[17] But since their arrival around 1370, the Franciscan Order managed to firmly establish itself in this region. They did help to contribute to the establishment of a diocesan seminary but kept the number of diocesan seminarians low while increasing their

---

15. Bogomil was a religion related to Manichaeism and spread to Western Europe where it was known as Albigensianism. In the twelfth century, surrounded by Orthodox and Latin Christians, the ruler of Bosnia asserted "a fuller independence" by adopting the Bogomil religion. Many Bosnians followed their ruler's example and were branded as heretics by the other Christians. See Andrić, *The Bridge Over The Drina*, 2.

16. Herrero, "Medjugorje," 144.

17. Rome's decision in 1923 which demanded that the Franciscans transfer some of their parishes to the diocesan clergy over a period of time, "far from constituting a secondary or irrelevant matter when approaching the Medjugorje movement from a socio-scientific perspective, the Herzegovina case holds important keys to understand the forces at work in Herzegovina's ethnic nationalism." Herrero, "Medjugorje," 143.

own numbers through well-organized vocation campaigns.[18] Thus at the beginning of the 1940s, the diocese of Mostar was still in the hands of the Franciscans while the diocesan clergy were relatively small in numbers. Even after World War II and the establishment of the communist regime in Yugoslavia, which resulted in the loss of properties, schools, and hospitals, the Franciscans remained influential in the region.

During the 1960s, the relationship between church and state had improved as each party realized the importance of working together for their own survival. Diplomatic relations between Rome and Yugoslavia were renewed in 1966. Supportive of the state government, the Bishop of Mostar, Janco Vladec, believed that Christianity and Marxism could coexist. In fact, Vladec recognized priests' associations established by the government and encouraged his clergy to join because he could foresee the benefits of such cooperation. Signing a secret agreement, which eventually became public, with the Bosnia Hercegovina authorities in 1966, the prelate was able to procure educational grants from the government for his diocese in exchange for state control over the selection of seminarians and appointment of parish priests.[19]

In 1965, the bishop was able to convince Rome to allow him to take over twenty-one of the sixty-three Franciscan parishes under his care. The Vatican named the first non-Franciscan Bishop of Mostar only in the twentieth century. In 1967, twelve more Franciscan parishes came under his jurisdiction, thus leaving the OFM with only thirty parishes.[20] Such a move won Vladec the support of middle class Catholics but incurred the wrath of the poor peasants who were anti-government. The transfer of the parishes from the Franciscans to the diocesan clergy was not smooth, to say the least. In some cases, conflicts between Franciscans and diocesan priests broke out in public.

In 1975, Rome wanted to give five more Franciscan parishes to the diocesan clergy. These five parishes belonged to the Franciscans since ancient times and they provided the source of their new vocation recruitment—it was their lifeline. Needless to say, the friars fought hard to keep these five parishes and Father Provincial was suspended for trying to intervene in Rome. The Bishop of Mostar interpreted it as an excommunication and declared the presence of the Franciscans in these parishes as contrary to

18. Bax, "Medjugorje," 64.
19. Ibid., 12.
20. Ibid.

canon law.[21] The friars could not evangelize non-believers without getting into trouble with the authorities and now they were left without any pastoral work. The Franciscans were in dire straits; only a miracle would save them.

Queen of Peace

Inspired by the Charismatic Renewal in Italy in 1979, Fr. Branko OFM who had served in Medjugorje for many years was assured that the Blessed Virgin Mary would help the Franciscans to maintain their presence there. Returning to Medjugorje, Branko started to organize catechism classes for children and women, and insisted on fasting, prayers, confession, and the recitation of the rosary. He was convinced that God would shower his special grace on the children of Medjugorje. When two village children were seriously ill, Branko formed prayer groups and kept vigil over them. On September 8, the feast of the Virgin's birth, the children recovered after intensive prayers. As a sign of gratitude, a special devotion to the Virgin Mary was set up in Medjugorje.[22]

The crucial moment arrived on June 24, 1981, when after attending Mass, six young children, ranging in age from ten to seventeen, Jakov Colo, Ivan Dragicevic, Mirjana Dragicevic, Ivanka Ivankovic, Vicka Ivankovic, and Marija Pavlovic, claimed to have seen a luminous figure on Podbrdo whom they believed to be *Gospa*, the Blessed Virgin Mary. The apparition was then reported to have occurred daily until March 1984, when the Virgin delivered a message at each apparition only once a month. From April 2001 onwards, only Marija Pavlovic, Vicki Ivankovic, and Ivan Dragicevic continued to experience a daily apparition. The rest were alleged to have received "ten secrets" from Our Lady and to have only one yearly apparition.[23]

Naturally, news of this incident spread like wildfire in the village. It was reported that *Gospa* was seen and heard by young visionaries, and she told them to pass this message to everyone: "peace and forbearance" among God's people.[24] This has been the recurring message till the present day. Called Queen of Peace, the Blessed Virgin urged people to pray, fast, confess, and receive communion. Prayer meetings in the evening at Podbrdo

21. Ibid., 13.
22. Ibid., 14.
23. Berryman, "Medjugorje's living icons," 597.
24. Bax, "Medjugorje," 65.

began to grow to a few thousand, and many reported having special graces, witnessing illumination, and being healed of their sickness.

Conflicts and Excommunication

Such new development unfortunately led to further conflicts and even persecutions by civil authorities. Later, there were conflicts between the Franciscans and the diocese, as well as the Vatican. The more the civil authorities tried to suppress this movement, the faster it grew. When the authorities prohibited visits to the mountains, the apparitions started again at different spots. The government campaign against the devotional movement only helped to publicize the apparitions at Medjugorje and encouraged more pilgrimages to the site. Two years later, the authorities became more accommodative to the growth of Medjugorje when the government realized that it made economic sense to allow pilgrims, especially those from abroad, to visit their beautiful mountains.

The conflict between the Franciscan and the civil authorities seemed to have abated but the tension with the Bishop Perić of Mostar escalated. This antagonism with the diocesan clergy only increased the devotional fervor of the people at Medjugorje. Unsuccessful in silencing the Franciscans, the bishop conducted an investigation on the apparitions with hope of exposing it as a hoax. Both Bishop Ratko Perić and the former Bishop of Mostar, Pavao Žanić, believed that the Franciscans masterminded the apparitions. His attempt to secure more parishes for his diocesan clergy antagonized the Franciscans, in particular two young friars, Ivica Vego and Ivan Prusina. Žanić was succeeded by Ratko Perić in 1993, who pursued the same policy of opposing the movement at Medjugorje.[25]

In a document published by the Mostar Chancery in 1984, Bishop Žanić declared that the apparitions at Medjugorje are nothing but "a case of collective hallucination" which was being "cleverly exploited by a group of Franciscans from Herzegovina" to tell simple folks that Our Lady supported them in the division of the parishes. The bishops added that the Franciscans' determination "to assert themselves in order to defend their position in the notorious 'Hercegovina case' as well as important material gain has eliminated all barriers and consideration"[26]

---

25. Herrero, "Medjugorje," 144.
26. Ibid., 151.

Žanić's successor, Bishop Perić, thus forbade Catholics in his diocese to make pilgrimages to Medjugorje and denied the sacraments to those who broke this rule. There were already many worshippers from his diocese at Medjugorje. Being denied the sacraments by the bishop in his parishes only drove them in huge numbers to the Franciscan parishes. In fact, the Franciscan parishes grew at such rapid rate that they needed more priests. As a result, the number of Franciscan priests working in the diocese of Mostar reached more than 120 in 1989.[27]

Perić reacted to this expansion by attempting to have the Franciscans arrested by accusing them and their relatives of involvement in nationalistic movements.[28] Such a reprisal only increased the devotional fervor of Medjugorje: nationalism became fused with the devotional movement. Highly respected, the persecuted Franciscans were regarded as political martyrs. In vain, the bishop also tried to show that the devotion promoted by the Franciscans in Medjugorje was a deviation from church's teachings.

As an international organization, the Franciscans were able to garner support and assistance from their worldwide network of friars, sisters, and lay associates. They invited experts to testify to the apparitions, and pilgrimages were organized from all over the world to Medjugorje. These pilgrims helped to spread the divine message from Our Lady of Medjugorje. Doctors and medical experts from the West were invited to study the cases of miraculous healing and their positive results were published widely. It was also reported that the Virgin Mary, in one of her messages, had urged the Bishop of Mostar to reconcile publicly with the Franciscans for he had wrongfully excommunicated a number of them. The Vatican was not left out: the Virgin announced that she loved the pope and supported him in his travels and his promotion of peace in the world.[29]

---

27. Bax, "Medjugorje," 65.

28. Led by Ante Pavelić, the so-called Independent State of Croatia came into existence in 1941. Under Pavelić, the Ustaše Militia committed atrocities against the Bosnian Serbs who were Orthodox Christians and attempted to convert another third to Catholicism with the aim of turning them into Croats. There were a number of Franciscans involved in this Ustaše genocide and forced conversions. Herrero, "Medjugorje," 141.

29. Bax, "Medjugorje," 68.

Secular Interpretations

What started off as a private experience of six young people in a remote village in Eastern Europe has now been transformed into a global phenomenon with international branches and networks—Medjugorje has become the geographical center of this worldwide movement. The struggle between the mendicant orders and diocesan clergy is not a new occurrence in the history of the Catholic Church, and sadly, some may interpret the promotion of Marian devotion as a strategy against diocesan encroachment into Franciscan territory. In other words, apparitions are seen as the result of the struggle between the regular and secular clergies. After all, both parties depend on the same faithful for their survival, and thus factionalism and competition are inevitable. In fact, Durkheim argues that "the sacred is the socially produced symbolic representation of society" and Weber holds that "the divine and its alleged manifestations entertain a mimetic relationship with society."[30] This suggests that the apparitions at Medjugorje were projections of a sorely needed solution to resolve the conflicts and tension that occurred in that locality.

From an ethnic-political point of view, "divine presence itself, as a source of unquestionable authority, became for the Herzegovinian Croats the most powerful argument to validate their nationalistic claims while infusing a renewed sense of righteousness in the population."[31] Cynics and critics have emphasized the economic miracles that took place, such as the rapid development of transportation, accommodation, restaurants, and souvenir shops, to cater for the needs of the pilgrims pouring in from all over world. In fact, government authorities realized the economic benefits of apparitions and encouraged foreign pilgrims to visit the sites so that it would not be transformed into a Croatian national shrine.[32] Our Lady of Medjugorje is now a mother of us all.

For those who have experienced conversion in Medjugorje, the fruits of the Holy Spirit are visible: "You will know them by their fruits" (Matt 7:16). One of the inhabitants of Medjugorje summed it up this way: "Since *Gospa* came here for the first time, vendettas have stopped and families are reunited. We are happy and well off, and we try to be friendly and hospitable. That is what Our Lady teaches us: we must be an example for the

---

30. Berryman, "Medjugorje's living icons," 594.
31. Herrero, "Medjugorje," 139.
32. Ramet, "The miracle at Medjugorje," 172.

world."[33] In the following section are two personal testimonies narrated by Aki and Michelle, friends of mine. They reveal the profound experiences and spiritual fruits gathered by those who have encountered the Madonna there.

Closer to Heaven

Aki, a close friend, holds the opinion that although Medjugorje is famous for miracles, she was against the idea of searching for or verifying miracles. She simply wanted to be there and see for herself what this place was all about. As a Christian, she believes our faith in God should rule every aspect of our lives, and we must acknowledge our need for God, as we tend to forget his real presence in our mundane lives.

All activities seen in Medjugorje and thousands of testimonies of conversion of hearts point to the reality that people's faith and hearts are changed after being there. One will most likely hear about some miraculous phenomena, if not experience some there. However, it was the enrichment of each person's internal life that has impressed Aki the most, and has continued to inspire her on her spiritual journey.

With pressing daily life obligations, finding time to be with God can be a luxury for many. Our Lady of Peace in Medjugorje constantly reminds Aki to spend more time in prayer. Of the many alleged wonders of Medjugorje, the strongest impression Aki had was about prayer.

Praying outwardly is not common in our world outside of Medjugorje. This usually only happens inside churches. The rare prayer scene we see sometimes is before meals. Medjugorje is an opposite reality, as Aki's first impression was its serenity and strong sense of community prayer—in each corner one can see groups, big or small, united in vocal prayer. There may be a group praying the rosary and singing together on the way to the Apparition Mountain or Cross Mountain. Seeing companionship in this way is inspirational and especially comforting for those who feel alone in their spiritual journey.

Before going to Medjugorje for the first time, Aki had kept a regular prayer routine. She was also part of an active church choir, being aware of "he who sings prays twice." Aki writes: "Thinking that I had sufficient connection with God through my prayers, when I saw the active prayer scenes everywhere in Medjugorje, I understood that our connection with

---

33. Bax, "Medjugorje," 69.

Power of Popular Piety

God through prayer can never be exhausted. As our entire being came from our mighty Creator, it is essential that our heart and soul are always connected with our Creator in order to have optimal experience in our lives by submitting to his will."

Our Lady's message of "pray, pray, pray" as a solution to our world's problems may seem radical and impractical to the unfaithful. However, Aki says, those who follow this advice with faith will not run short of testimonies of how following this advice in fact enhanced lives. In Medjugorje, one can start by being part of this prayer oasis.

Our spiritual needs are also being taken care of through confessions in Medjugorje, according to Aki. She observes that many practicing Catholics think that confession once a month may be good enough, while some speeches by exorcists reveal that more frequent confessions, especially of venial sins, are most beneficial for a soul to remain in God's grace. For Aki, Medjugorje is a place where one will see grace in visible form through the Sacrament of Penance. Confession is recommended to be the first thing you do upon arriving so that your soul will be cleansed before receiving and retaining blessings there.

Scenes of prayers were inspiring, but the confession area was truly touching. The confession area is filled with courage and grace, as it takes courage and faith in God to bare your soul to the confessor. Although Aki could not see inside each person's heart, she saw the return of many prodigal sons and daughters through this exercise in Medjugorje. The reconciliation and healing that resulted from confessions left strong impressions in Aki's heart.

After experiencing the serenity and grace through prayers, confessions, celebration of the Eucharist, and other experiences and encounters, Aki returns to the "real world" with a soul that is recharged. It is said that not only is the experience in Medjugorje valuable, but very often the fruits of the experience appear only after the trip. Aki points out that this truly is a mystery and for those who have faith in God, there is no need to understand everything completely. In a faithful traveller's journey, making a stop in Medjugorje refreshes the soul and equips it with spiritual weapons for the journey toward our home in heaven. Aki feels closer to heaven when in Medjugorje. For this reason alone, the ticket to Medjugorje for Aki was well worth the cost.

Heaven Touches Earth

Since her first visit to Medjugorje in 2000, Michelle has been accompanying pilgrims there. In fact, since 2002, she has been bringing groups twice or three times a year. It is now a full-time service for her. She admits that she has had some personal encounters with Our Lady, but not many. However, Michelle has witnessed how the Virgin has worked on each person: "I just need to bring the people to her, which often also lets me encounter Jesus in a special way in every pilgrimage. I never return home from Medjugorje with empty hands." She continues, "Every time I step into Medjugorje, I realize the need for conversion within me."

Michelle narrates this story to me. Patrick was a retired French medical doctor who went to Medjugorje for the first time at the age of sixty. Suffering from depression, he described himself as a sad person. In Medjugorje, like every pilgrim, he climbed Podbrdo (now known as the Apparition Hill, where the Blessed Virgin appeared). He was shocked to see such a prayerful place filled with so much rubbish and garbage. He began to collect all the rubbish in his own bag, in order to bring it to the bins.

While he was collecting the rubbish he heard a voice in his heart telling him, "Perhaps, it will be better if you clean the rubbish in your heart." The voice repeated twice, and he finally sat down and prayed. Suddenly he recalled an incident that had happened when he was still a student doctor at the age of twenty.

At that time, Patrick was visiting an old lady in the ward. He wanted to give her an injection to reduce her pain. At the same time, he knew very well there was a high probability that this injection might kill her. Anyway, he just wanted to test it to see how effective this injection was, without thinking of the dire consequences. He did not consult any doctor or nurse. Two hours after the injection, this old lady passed away. Patrick did not feel any remorse about this incident, as he just wanted to know if the injection would work or not.

It was on the Apparition Hill, sitting in front of the statue, in prayer, that the Lord reminded him that he had killed the old lady. Patrick rushed to the parish to make his confession, of a sin that he had committed forty years ago.

Michelle continued and said, "Indeed, many times we have lost the sense of good or evil. We take the goodness of the Lord for granted." Thus it is important that we examine our conscience in prayer regularly so that the Lord will enlighten and dispel the darkness in our hearts. After Patrick went for his confession, he testified that the sadness he had carried for so many years disappeared. The depression was gone.

Since the beginning of the apparition on June 24, 1981, the parish of Medjugorje has held a three-hour prayer session daily in the church, with the local inhabitants and the pilgrims. During special seasons like in early August, when the International Youth Prayer Festival takes place, hundreds of priests from all different countries gather in this little village, to hear confessions in different languages. This event has been held in Medjugorje for more than twenty-five years.

This special grace of confessions in Medjugorje has resulted in many physical and spiritual healings, according to Michelle. Confession is truly the remedy for the sick humanity of this time. When we acknowledge our own weaknesses, our hatred and resentment, and then offer them to the Lord in confession, grace will be granted to us. It will restore peace in our hearts. Aki feels closer to heaven when she is in Medjugorje. Michelle says she experiences Medjugorje as a place where heaven touches the earth.

Common Characteristics

French theologian René Laurentin arrived in Medjugorje in December 1983 to observe the vision and arrived at the following conclusions:

1. The vision begins the same way consistently: it appears that the children see something, they are joyful and they fall on their knees. They gaze at a fixed point.
2. During the vision, they speak with someone whose voice is not heard.
3. During this time, they are withdrawn from their surrounding world. When the vision was over, they were not aware of it.
4. The witnesses are convinced that they see the Virgin Mary as a person that they can touch.
5. They believe that the Mother of God is speaking to them but no one else can hear.
6. They hear voices after two to three minutes and then they continue to pray the Our Father but one does not hear the first words, "Our Father."

7. Finally when this joyful vision ends, the children are not disappointed but are prepared to face any difficulties and challenges in life. They continue to pray fervently and fast twice a week. They are able to face threats and bear the burden of sympathy with calmness.[34]

In cooperation with a medical doctor Henry Joyeux, Laurentin published scientific and medical reports in support of the vision at Medjugorje in his 1985 book, *Scientific and Medical Studies on the Apparitions at Medjugorje*. Local doctors had subjected the children to various medical tests and mental health observations but found no sign of pathology. More comprehensive studies were done in 1984 by a team of Italian and French medical specialists and psychiatrists sponsored by the University of Montpellier. The seers consented to the tests after seeking permission from the Virgin. Joyeux and the Montpellier team confirmed that the children were mentally and physically healthy; they were not experiencing hallucination and showed no signs of collective hysteria.[35] In spite of the inconclusive result, Laurentin is convinced that Mary has visited the children.

The children were not particularly pious before the vision, but after this experience, they became very devout and manifested a deep growth in their spiritual life, while retaining the same personality and character. Another important development is that the parish experienced a profound spiritual renewal with the faithful praying the rosary fervently. The village parish is simply given to prayer and the pilgrims experience a deep conversion.

The Quest for Peace

Bosnia was once "a model of a multicultural, multiethnic, and multireligious community" and symbolized what was ideal during Tito and post-Tito Yugoslavia.[36]

However, unscrupulous and power-hungry politicians in the 1990s preached a nationalist ideology that split the region into various warring factions. Thus, post-Tito Yugoslavia was broken into the republics of Croatia, Slovenia, Macedonia, and Serbia-Montenegro, while Bosnia-Hercegovina was divided further into Croat-Muslim and Serb republics.

---

34. Cebulski, "Medjugorje," 143.
35. Herrero, "Medjugorje," 148–49
36. Gruenwald, "The Bridge to Eternity," 131–32.

Bosnian theologian and political scientist Rev. Marko Oršolić, OFM, is critical of a nationalism that attempts to merge the state and the church to serve secular ends. Supportive of ecumenism, he asserts that Catholicism and Orthodoxy are one and the same faith in spite of theological differences. He also believes that Christians, Muslims, Jews, and adherents of other religions can live together in peace and harmony in the Balkans and elsewhere.[37] Theological and doctrinal differences should not prevent us from pursuing this goal of unity in diversity. In the end, we are answerable to God and not to nations, ideologies, human-made religious dogmas and traditions.

Convinced that Bosnia could have been an anticipation of a Europe that is capable of dialogue and tolerance, Oršolić laments that today it is not just Bosnia that is being destroyed, but the whole of Europe. Nonetheless, Oršolić believes that the ecumenical spirit of Medjugorje, with its message of universal peace and forbearance, is perhaps the West's best hope for reconciling differences of belief and culture.

The apparitions of the Blessed Virgin Mary to a group of children since June 1981 proclaim a message that is more relevant than ever in our divided world: the infinite love of God for all men and women regardless of their religious belief or lack of belief; the need to repent, to be converted, and to forgive as a necessary condition for inner peace and peace in the world. The ecumenical message of Medjugorje is also biblical: "return to God, believe, and reform your life."[38] This message, pray and repent, is not just for Catholics but also for all people of goodwill.

Queen of Peace

Does the civil war that occurred ten years after the first apparition invalidate the message of Medjugorje? Some believe the message of Our Lady actually prepares us for such calamity. There is a difference between inner peace and outer peace. Inner or spiritual peace can exist in a person living in a war-torn country. Some people feel spiritually peaceful and liberated even when they are in prison. The peace of God surpasses all understanding. Christ says: "Peace I leave with you; my peace I give to you. I do not give to you as the world gives. Do not let your hearts be troubled, and do

---

37. Ibid., 140.
38. Ibid., 141.

not let them be afraid." (John 14:27) This inner peace is precisely the message of Medjugorje proclaimed by Mary, Queen of Peace.

Wars and conflicts occur all the time due to our fallen nature. But Christ promises inner peace if we put our trust in him: "I have said this to you, so that in me you may have peace. In the world you face persecution. But take courage; I have conquered the world!" (John 16:33) The civil war in Yugoslavia does not invalidate the message of Medjugorje, but only confirms the relevance and urgency of its warning—to pray and repent in order to achieve lasting peace.

Given in a particular place, the message of Medjugorje has a universal significance and a global implication. It proclaims the need for a moral regeneration and spiritual renewal for all humankind. Medjugorje thus is an "icon" or "bridge" between God and human beings, with Mary, the Mother of God, as its messenger imploring all of us to, pray, repent, and return to God.[39] Not just a particular Croatian phenomenon, Medjugorje has become an international movement, and its Christian message is ecumenical and universal.

Many people have visited Medjugorje, perhaps for different reasons, and most returned with a profound sense of having been touched by God through Our Lady. In a remote corner of this earth, they have witnessed God's grace speaking through simple people. The apparitions first witnessed by six young people have transformed Medjugorje into an oasis of peace where Orthodox, Catholics, Protestants, Jews, and Muslims meet as brothers and sisters. The message of Mary is always the same: conversion, prayer, and fasting: "I am the mother of all, whether Muslim, Orthodox, or Catholic. All are my children."[40] A different world is indeed possible.

In the next chapter, we will discuss how veneration of the Sacred Heart of Jesus has been replaced by devotion to the Divine Mercy, which like the devotion to the Virgin of Medjugorje, is more ecumenical and universal in its appeal.

---

39. Ibid., 145.
40. Muse, "The Bridge Keeper," 50.

Chapter 7

Sacred Heart and Divine Mercy

> The heart has its reasons which reason knows nothing of...
> We know the truth not only by the reason, but by the heart.
>
> —Blaise Pascal[1]

No symbol portrays divine love and compassion so powerfully and attracts such widespread devotion as the image of the Sacred Heart of Jesus. It all began in 1672 when a young nun, Margaret Mary Alacoque (1647–90), was reported to have received four revelations in which Jesus showed her his Sacred Heart and asked her to promote it publicly. Almost 300 years later in 1931, Jesus appeared again to another young nun in Poland, Faustina Kowalska, and revealed himself as Divine Mercy.

We shall discuss these two popular forms of devotion to Jesus—Sacred Heart and Divine Mercy—and see how they cater to the spiritual needs of the faithful at different times in history. The two devotions cannot be separated because Jesus has only one heart, full of love and mercy. Just as Margaret Mary Alacoque's revelations of the Sacred Heart were urgently needed between the seventeenth and nineteenth centuries, the life and witness of Faustina Kowalska was a gift of God for our time.

---

1. Pascal, *Pensées*: "The heart has its reasons, which reason does not know. We feel it in a thousand things. I say that the heart naturally loves the Universal Being, and also itself naturally, according as it gives itself to them; and it hardens itself against one or the other at its will. You have rejected the one and kept the other. Is it by reason that you love yourself? It is the heart which experiences God, and not the reason. This, then, is faith: God felt by the heart, not by the reason." Ibid., 277–78.

Jesus explained to the nun Alacoque that his heart burned for all creation and he promised mercy, compassion, and love to everyone who comes to him. Unfortunately, many people, including Christians, have neglected him. Jesus requested Alacoque to show her affection by receiving communion frequently, especially on the first Friday of each month, spending an hour in adoration of the Blessed Sacrament on Thursday night, and offering sacrifices for the sins of the world. Jesus also encouraged the nun to promote the veneration of his Sacred Heart as a Feast Day of the church. This Feast will be celebrated by the faithful by receiving Holy Communion and asking his blessings. Devotion to the Sacred Heart of Jesus would be rewarded with special acts of grace for the individuals as well as for members of their families. This love is symbolized by Jesus' inflamed heart.

The basis for devotion to the heart of Jesus can be found in Scripture and in the teaching of St. Thomas Aquinas. It was promoted by Francis de Sales, cofounder of the Order of Visitation with Jeanne de Chantal. De Sales describes to Chantal the image of the heart as a symbol of the new order.

Biblical Background

In the Old Testament, the word heart occurs approximately a thousand times and in the New Testament, it occurs around 150 times. "Heart" is associated with thinking, understanding, knowledge, and wisdom. It touches the core of the person's existence: "Make the heart of this people fat . . . and understand with their hearts, and turn and be healed" (Isa 6: 10). When Jesus was presented in the temple, "Simeon blessed them, and said to Mary his mother, Behold, this Child is destined for the fall and rising of many in Israel, and for a sign which will be spoken against (yes, a sword will pierce through your own soul also), that the thoughts of many hearts may be revealed" (Luke 2:34–35); "But Mary treasured all these words and pondered them in her heart" (Luke 2:19). Jesus said to his disciples, "Why are you frightened, and why do doubts arise in your hearts?" (Luke 24:38) In Scripture, a person of the heart is one who is wise and perceptive.

Faith is also a matter of the heart: "For one believes with the heart and so is justified, and one confesses with the mouth and so is saved" (Rom 10:10); "For it is the God who said, 'Let light shine out of darkness,' who has shone in our hearts to give the light of the knowledge of the glory of God in the face of Jesus Christ" (2 Cor 4:6); "so that, with the eyes of your heart enlightened, you may know what is the hope to which he has called you, what are the riches of his glorious inheritance among the saints" (Eph 1: 18); "and that Christ may dwell in your hearts through faith, as you are being rooted and grounded in love" (Eph 3: 17). The person's heart can be understood in terms of the "inner disposition of his will" and the source of all that is good and true.[2]

Piercing of the Side of Jesus

According to Scripture, John the disciple plays a crucial role in the development of devotion to the Heart of Jesus. At the Last Supper, John was lying close to Jesus' breast (John 13: 25), which signifies that he "rested in Jesus's innermost heart and in the inner meaning of his teaching," according to Origen.[3] The Johannine image of the pierced Savior is of great soteriological significance.[4]

> Since it was the day of Preparation, the Jews did not want the bodies left on the cross during the Sabbath, especially because that Sabbath was a day of great solemnity. So they asked Pilate to have the legs of the crucified men broken and the bodies removed. Then the soldiers came and broke the legs of the first and of the other who had been crucified with him. But when they came to Jesus and saw that he was already dead, they did not break his legs. Instead, one of the soldiers pierced his side with a spear, and at once blood and water came out. (John 19:31–34)

Taking the *pierced side* and *love* together conjures an image of the "Pierced Heart of Jesus," corresponding to the devotion to the Heart of Jesus.[5]

---

2. Becker, "The Heart in the Language of the Bible," 27.
3. Baier, "Key Issues in Medieval Sacred Heart Piety," 83.
4. Heer, "The Soteriological Significance of the Johannine Image of the Pierced Savior," 33–46.
5. Ibid., 45.

Adoration and Veneration

Thomas Aquinas treats the question of devotion to Christ by distinguishing between adoration or worship (*latria*) reserved only for God and veneration (*dulia*) for creatures. Veneration is given to the entire person, even if we have devotion to the Sacred Heart of Jesus. We worship Christ as the incarnate Word of God and venerate Jesus in our devotion to his most Sacred Heart:

> And so the adoration of Christ's humanity may be understood in two ways. First, so that the humanity is the thing adored: and thus to adore the flesh of Christ is nothing else than to adore the incarnate Word of God ... Secondly, the adoration of Christ's humanity may be taken as given by reason of its being perfected with every gift of grace. And so in this sense the adoration of Christ's humanity is the adoration not of "latria" but of "dulia." So that one and the same Person of Christ is adored with "latria" on account of His Divinity, and with "dulia" on account of His perfect humanity.[6]

Thomas uses the word *cor* (heart) to mean the "vital principle of animal life and of movement" as well as the "organ of passions." There is a correspondence between the love of Jesus and his physical heart in the sense that the heart is the "principle of bodily movement."[7] Love is the motivating force behind all of Christ's actions. In the veneration of Jesus as a man, Thomas focuses not on individual parts of his physical body but on his love for us.

Love that is Affective and Effective

Francis de Sales's theology of the heart emphasizes the relationship between prayer and love, a love that is both affective and effective. For those who have not built a deep prayer life, it is difficult to understand Francis de Sales's *Treaties on the Love of God*. De Sales's theology is a "prayed dogmatics," a theology of mysticism and spirituality: "he touches the most intimate relationships between God and the human soul, the mysterious ways of what, for lack of a better expression, we call 'grace.'" The emphasis here is on the personal experience of God's love and thus a believer has to be "mystic."

---

6. Aquinas, *Summa Theologica*, III.25, 2.

7. Elders, "The Inner Life of Jesus in the Theology and Devotion of Saint Thomas Aquinas," 79.

In his letter to Jeanne de Chantal, de Sales writes, "I confess my opinion that no man loves more fervently, more tenderly—frankly that no one is more in love—than I. But it has pleased God to give me such a heart."[8]

Regarding the founding of the Order of Visitation, Francis de Sales writes to Chantal the cofounder, advising her to anchor the sisters' spirituality on the love of God expressed in the heart of Jesus: ". . . we shall take as our device a single Heart, pierced by two arrows and encircled with a crown of thorns. This poor Heart, engraved with the sacred names of Jesus and Mary and surmounted by a cross, shall be our sign . . . our little Congregation is the work of the Hearts of Jesus and Mary. By opening his Sacred Heart in death the Savior has given us his life."[9] In the heart of Jesus, the love of God is revealed to us, Francis de Sales teaches.

Furnace of Ardent Love

Margaret Mary Alacoque, a nun of the Order of the Visitation of Mary at Paray-le-Monial, France, claimed that Jesus appeared to her between 1673 and 1675. Jesus expressed to Alacoque his burning love for humankind in vivid imagery:

> My Divine Heart is so inflamed with love for men, and for you in particular that, being unable any longer to contain within Itself the flames of Its burning Charity, It must needs spread them abroad by your means, and manifest Itself to them (humankind) in order to enrich them with the precious graces of sanctification and salvation necessary to withdraw them from the abyss of perdition. I have chosen you as an abyss of unworthiness and ignorance for the accomplishment of this great design, in order that everything may be done by Me.[10]

Alacoque added that the divine Heart of Jesus was revealed to her as presented on a throne of flames that is brighter than the sun, and encircled by a crown of thorns surmounted by a cross. The wounds that Jesus received on the cross also appeared vividly:

> On one occasion, while the Blessed Sacrament was exposed, feeling wholly withdrawn within myself by an extraordinary recollection

---

8. Mattes, "Devotion to the Heart of Jesus in Modern Times," 103.
9. Ibid.,104.
10. *Catholic Culture*.

of all my senses and powers, Jesus Christ, my sweet Master, presented Himself to me, all resplendent with glory, His Five Wounds shining like so many suns. Flames issued from every part of His Sacred Humanity, especially from His Adorable Breast, which resembled an open furnace and disclosed to me His most loving and most amiable Heart, which was the living source of these flames. It was then that He made known to me the ineffable marvels of His pure love and showed me to what an excess He had loved men, from whom He received only ingratitude and contempt.[11]

In another vision revealed to Alacoque, Christ requested that a special Feast be established to honor his heart. Like the previous one, this revelation occurred before the Blessed Sacrament where Jesus exposed his Sacred Heart to her and said:

Behold the Heart which has so loved men that it has spared nothing, even to exhausting and consuming Itself, in order to testify Its love; and in return, I receive from the greater part only ingratitude, by their irreverence and sacrilege, and by the coldness and contempt they have for Me in this Sacrament of Love. But what I feel most keenly is that it is hearts which are consecrated to Me, that treat Me thus. Therefore, I ask of you that the Friday after the Octave of Corpus Christi be set apart for a special Feast to honor My Heart, by communicating on that day, and making reparation to It by a solemn act, in order to make amends for the indignities which It has received during the time It has been exposed on the altars. I promise you that My Heart shall expand Itself to shed in abundance the influence of Its Divine Love upon those who shall thus honor It, and cause It to be honored.[12]

Alacoque told her community of nuns that Jesus showed her his Sacred Heart during his many visits. The image she saw was sketched on a paper showing Jesus' heart pierced by a lance, circled by thorns and flames and surmounted with a cross. With this mystical experience Alacoque promoted the devotion with much zeal and enthusiasm, with the support of her religious community and a few Jesuit priests including her confessors. She wrote and published retreat manuals and devotional guides, and she sketched emblematic images of the Sacred Heart that were modified a few times to suit different places and purposes.

---

11. Ibid.
12 Ibid.

During the last seventeen years of her life, Alacoque was completely dedicated to promoting the Sacred Heart of Jesus. Between 1673 and 1685, she attempted to interpret her visions and wrote these in her autobiography. From 1685 to 1687, Alacoque was occupied with spreading the message of the Sacred Heart while directing the novices in her community. With the assistance of the novices, Alacoque was able to transform her private devotion into a communal one. Later the devotion to the Sacred Heart spread to the other convents in her order. Finally from 1688 to the end of her life in 1690, Alacoque consolidated her ideas of the Sacred Heart in an authoritative text with the help of Fr. Croiset.

During this last stage of her life, Alacoque received a revelation in which Jesus asked that the King of France, Louis XIV, consecrate himself and his nation to the Sacred Heart, but unfortunately, the request was not acted upon. Not until two violent revolutions had taken place in France did a Basilica at Montmartre in Paris get built as a symbol of the nation's consecration to the Heart of Jesus. Alacoque suffered great physical and spiritual trials while promoting the devotion to the Sacred Heart. Through her sacrifices and prayers, the devotion spread throughout the world after much oppositions, as we shall see. This popular piety was promoted from the pulpit to the political sphere.

Private to Public

Devotion to the Sacred Heart played a prominent role in the politics of France. Cloth images of the Sacred Heart were sewn to the uniforms of the French volunteers fighting against the Republicans: "With the Sacré-Coeur stitched to their uniforms, they became the embodiment of a Christian patriotism and testified to their belief in an ongoing struggle against the Revolution."[13] In fact, Alacqoue's vision became politicized when in the 1680s Jesus was alleged to have told her to make the Sacred Heart an official devotion. By means of consecration to the Sacred Heart, the king of France would receive grace and glory in a world divided by heresy and political conflicts. The culmination of this popular piety was the construction of the Basilica of the Sacred Heart of Jesus of Montmartre in the 1880s as mentioned above.

The early images of the Sacred Heart were symbolic in nature, rather than a physical portrayal of the human heart. However, the dominant

---

13. Jonas, *France and the Cult of the Sacred Heart*, 161.

Sacred Heart and Divine Mercy

iconography in the following century would be visceral, relating to the heart as an organ in the body. Alacoque would later write to Croiset: "It must be honored under the symbol of this Heart of flesh, Whose image He wished to be publicly exposed. He wanted me to carry it on my person, over my heart, that He might imprint His love there, fill my heart with all the gifts with which His own is filled, and destroy all inordinate affection. Wherever this sacred image would be exposed for veneration He would pour forth His graces and blessings."[14] The promotion of this image and its message started a chain of reactions in criticism, defensiveness, and finally, enthusiastic reception.

Controversies and conflicts started when the heart was viewed by the faithful as a separate object on its own. This was not what the devotion is about, according to Church teaching. In fact the mystery of the Sacred Heart encompasses the entire person of Christ and his heart is a natural symbol of his all-embracing love. Thus, from the time it became popular, it was also debated and attacked from within and without the Church. Her community at Paray-le-Monial was probably the first to oppose such veneration because it was "a new devotion."[15] Criticisms of the devotion to the Sacred Heart came from the Jansenists and defense came from the Jesuits, both groups being influential and prominent in France in the eighteenth century. In 1696, a Jesuit, Joseph de Gallifet, submitted to Rome a work on the "Veneration of the Most Sacred Heart of Jesus," but it was approved only three years after his death in 1741. Rome initially did not approve of the Devotion to the Sacred Heart of Jesus for three reasons:

> 1. It was a New Feast, and there were insufficient grounds for its introduction.
>
> 2. There would have to be an initial judicial examination concerning Sister Margaret Alacoque, who was responsible for the whole issue.
>
> 3. Gallifet's view, according to which the heart was the seat of love and all the emotions, was highly disputed, since modern philosophy attributed these activities to the brain.[16]

---

14. Morgan, *The Sacred Heart of Jesus*, 12.
15. Ibid., 5.
16. Mattes, "Devotion to the Heart of Jesus in Modern Times," 109.

Power of Popular Piety
Jesuits and Jansenists

As a counter-Reformation movement, the Jesuits attempted to halt the spread of Protestantism in Europe and to promote the interests of the Catholic Church. In France, the principal Protestants were the Huguenots, a Calvinist sect, for whom freedom to practice their religion had been guaranteed by the Edict of Nantes. In 1685, Louis XVI revoked the Edict of Nantes in the hope that the Huguenots would convert to Catholicism and thus help to unite a divided country. Alacoque also hoped that through Devotion to the Sacred Heart the Huguenots would be converted.[17]

The Jansenists also pursued the counter-Reform movement by adopting a different theological approach. The Jesuits extended the influence of Catholicism by assimilating the humanism of the Renaissance, whereas the Jansenists integrated elements of Calvinism with the hope of attracting Protestants like the Huguenots back to the Catholic fold.[18]

Jansenism was a movement started by Bishop Cornelius Jansen of Ypres (1585–1638) for the purpose of reviving Christian life with strict and austere lifestyle. This group lamented the decline of morals and blamed the Church authorities for the laxity in spiritual life among Catholics. Based on the theology of St. Augustine, Jansenists imposed strict rules and disciplines, and emphasized the wrath and justice of God. Consisting of intellectuals from the Netherlands, France, and Italy (including the scientist and philosopher Blaise Pascal), Jansenists held a very narrow understanding of salvation. In other words, in their interpretation only a few elects would be saved and redeemed by God. This theology espoused by Jansenism was a threat to the power of the papacy, which alone, it believed, has jurisdiction over spiritual matters.

The Jesuits who pledged a special loyalty to the pope were naturally against the Calvinistic tendency of Jansenism. A sharp contrast existed between Jesuit Baroque spirituality and the austerity of Jansenism. Devotion to the Sacred Heart of Jesus finds a natural ally in the humanism of Jesuit spirituality. Claude de la Colombière, a young Jesuit, was one of Alacoque's confessors in 1675. Colombière helped her to interpret her visions and to communicate their message to the world at large. In fact, Colombière became one of her strongest supporters—"Her cause became his. He relayed

---

17. Morgan, *The Sacred Heart of Jesus*, 12.
18. McManners, *Church and Society in Eighteenth-Century France*, 350.

her message to his superiors. The Sacré-Coeur became a Jesuit cause."[19] This validation by the Jesuits, a powerful and prestigious male religious order, gave Alacoque the recognition she needed from an established authority. Such an endorsement from the Society of Jesus served also to convince her superiors and other skeptics in her community of the truth of her vision.

Opposed to Jansenism, the Jesuits advocated devotion to the Sacred Heart of Jesus because this popular piety took seriously the grace given by Christ through his sacrificial love. Each person is called by God to repent, to make reparation for the offences against God. Penitential practices include receiving Holy Communion, going on a pilgrimage, praying the rosary, attending mass on feast days, and contemplating the images of the Sacred Heart of Jesus, the Immaculate Heart of Mary, and other saints. All these practices of piety will be rewarded with grace, favors, and blessings from God. They are to be regarded as the individuals' efforts to seek forgiveness from God for the sins they have committed. This kind of sensuous and benevolent devotion was totally against the austere teaching of Jansenism. The most controversial part of the devotion to the Sacred Heart was the presentation of the visceral heart in a simple, natural sense, and not as symbolic. Reparation was repaid by this devotion and also indulgences given by bishops and pope in 1692, two years after Alacoque's death. Thus, devotion to the Sacred Heart gained currency in the economics of salvation.[20]

Criticism of the devotion of the Sacred Heart of Jesus also came from Bishop Scipio de Ricci, who wanted to reduce the altars and images in the churches, and discouraged the use of indulgences. Ricci regarded devotion to the Sacred Heart as "womanish" practice in reference to the passionate nature of Alacoque's attachment to Jesus.[21] Ricci was also combating the tendency of appealing to the physical body in spirituality. Ricci dismissed the Devotion to the Sacred Heart as new and unnecessary, and advocated a more robust kind of devotion that focused on the Eucharist.

In spite of oppositions from various quarters within the Church, Pius VI in 1794 officially approved the devotion to the Sacred Heart and issued indulgences to those who practiced it. At the same time, the pope also issued a bull, *Auctorem Fidei*, condemning Jansenism and Ricci's teachings. Margaret Mary Alacoque was beatified by Pope Pius IX on September 18, 1864 and canonized by Pope Benedict XV on May 13, 1920.

19. Jonas, *France and the Cult of the Sacred Heart*, 24.
20. Morgan, *The Sacred Heart of Jesus*, 14.
21. Ibid., 18.

After Alacoque's beatification, devotion to the Sacred Heart spread rapidly to other churches in France, partly due to the images that could be produced economically. The direct gaze of Jesus as portrayed in the various images appealed to devotees in the nineteenth century. The images produced in inexpensive lithographic form appeared on prayer cards, posters and large portraits for display in churches. The femininity of Jesus, symbolized by his heart, also appeals to many people in the church—it reveals Jesus' tenderness, accessibility, and even vulnerability.[22] This intimate act of exposing his heart won many devotees.

Devotion to the Sacred Heart of Jesus has been enlisted as a bulwark against the French Revolution, communism, and threats to family life. In 1856, Pope Pius XI proclaimed this devotion a Feast of the universal Church, and in 1899, Leo XII consecrated the entire world to the Sacred Heart. The Church also designated June 8 as the Solemnity of the Sacred Heart of Jesus.

Decline of the Devotion

Devotion to the Sacred Heart of Jesus has suffered a "cardiac arrest" in recent decades and has been dismissed as superstitious and masochistic.[23] Some others regarded this pious practice as effeminate and saccharine. To stop this decline, a healthy diet of Scripture and tradition is needed to resuscitate this popular piety. The last important pronouncement by the Magisterium on the devotion to the Heart of Jesus is in the encyclical *Haurietis aquas* of Pius XII, which reveals a decline in the devotion and attempts to revive it. The devotion to the Sacred Heart has suffered from the weakness of its pietistic language and pictorial representation, and had lost its appeal to the new generation of Catholics. The devotion has experienced a "decline in the value of its language and concepts, false sentimentality and anemic artistic effort."[24]

This decline is also influenced by the christological debate, which in the last few decades has centered around the humanity and divinity of Jesus Christ, and by the prevalence of secularism in Western societies. Devotion to the Sacred Heart is no longer regarded as relevant to the needs of the church and humankind. It lies at the periphery of the Catholic faith and

---

22. Ibid., 22.
23. Ruddy, "The Sacred Heart of Jesus," 9.
24. Mattes, "Devotion to the Heart of Jesus in Modern Times," 114.

thus it is optional. It is seen as too passive and feminine, and therefore, of no use to the modern revival of faith. Some think the devotion is distorted by an erroneous mysticism.

To combat this decline, Hugo Rahner calls for a new study of the theological basis of this devotion, which in the past was obscured by shallow and sentimental piety. He focuses on the great mysteries of the Trinity and the incarnation as the fundamental form of the mystery of love. Rahner also emphasizes the eschatological dimension of devotion to the Sacred Heart of Jesus: "Every form of devotion shares with the Church that tension that arises between disappointment of the present and the longed-for future" and "in future the Devotion, earthly as it is, will have to manifest itself more clearly as the eschatological cult of the human and saving love of God . . . . The more a sense of eschatological mystery penetrates our contemporary devotional forms, the more biblical, theological and hence fruitful they will be."[25] This theological foundation has to be balanced by a spirituality that expresses Jesus' solidarity with humankind in more tangible forms. We also need to look for new symbols and imagery to revive our faith in Christ.

The devotion to the Heart of Jesus is in crisis, according to Josef Heer. Devotion to the Sacred Heart cannot be cultivated solely through the celebration of the Eucharist. It has to be given space in both the church liturgy as well as a popular piety—there must be room for a private and subjective devotion that transcends the official cult of the church. To revive this cult, we need more than just breathing new life into an old form. A new form has to be found that can convey the idea of *expiation* where persons can make up for the sins that they and others have committed.[26] In other words, we must emphasize the fundamental Christian truth that we are persons for others in solidarity with the poor, oppressed, and marginalized.

Many are clamoring for personal experience of the divine as revealed by the popularity of Pentecostalism, where people can feel the effects and fruits of the Holy Spirit. Leo Scheffczyk says the anamnesis-experience of Jesus, a recollection of past event, cannot be reduced to a mere remembrance. Christ's presence is guaranteed by the Holy Spirit—thus the person of Jesus Christ, the God-man is "pneumatised."[27] St. Paul says, "Now the Lord is the Spirit, and where the Spirit of the Lord is, there is freedom"

25. Ibid., 115.
26. Heer, "The Soteriological Significance of the Johannine Image of the Pierced Savior," 45.
27. Scheffczyk, "Devotion to Christ as a way of Experiencing him," 210.

(2 Cor 3:17). It is thus possible to experience the person of Jesus Christ because he is a divine person. At the same time, his divinity and humanity are inseparable and therefore our experience of him is of one person, divine and human. We can actually experience the human sufferings and pains of a person who is also God. This experience is even more powerful than if Jesus was merely a human being.

To experience Jesus Christ, we must have a proper disposition, an openness to the Spirit. This means that our relationship with Jesus must not be based merely according to our human needs and caprices: "Experience of the pneumatic Lord can only be made in an appropriate, Spirit-given openness and readiness. It determines the human, subjective structure of devotion. It is a pneumatic attitude of unreserved openness and receptivity vis-à-vis the Lord pneumatically present."[28] This openness to the Spirit's illumination will facilitate our meditation and contemplation of Jesus Christ.

Our new and restless generation is still searching for someone with a heart, someone who understands and cares. Perhaps, the devotion to Divine Mercy meets this need; through it we find that someone, Jesus, God and Man, who is in touch with the realities of our times, of all times. In the next section, we will discuss the devotion to Divine Mercy beginning with a brief sketch of its "apostle," St. Faustina Kowalska.

Life of Faustina

Helena Kowalska was born in the village of Glogowiec, Poland, in 1905. At the age of twenty, she entered the convent of the Sisters of Our Lady of Mercy and chose the name Sister Maria Faustina of the Most Blessed Sacrament. The Congregation of Our Lady of Mercy was founded by Teresa Rondeau in 1818 in Laval, France. In 1862, it was brought to Poland by Ewa (Sulkowska), Countess Potocka. The spirituality of this congregation was and still is the imitation of Christ in his mercy towards sinners; its specific mission is the rehabilitation of wayward girls.[29]

In the religious community, Faustina's prayer life deepened and she grew strong in her practice of Christian virtues. Since she had only two winters of education, Faustina did manual work as a cook, gardener, and potter for her community. She was attentive to the poor who came to her convent asking for food and she was also kind to the girls who were trained

---

28. Ibid., 211.
29. Michalenko, *The Life of Faustina Kowalska*, 29.

and educated by her religious congregation. Her holiness was known and many came to seek her advice and counsel.[30]

The Lord appeared and revealed his merciful heart to Faustina after she experienced a period of spiritual purification. She began to receive revelations, visions, and locutions, all based on the theme of the Lord's mercy for the lost and broken. Advised by her spiritual director, Faustina began to record her spiritual experiences in her *Diary*, which has become a spiritual classic of the twentieth century. This was considered a miracle by itself because Faustina had only two years of elementary education.

While she enjoyed mystical revelation, Faustina had also to endure physical ailments such as tuberculosis, which slowly began eating away her body. Most painful of all was the criticism from some of her fellow sisters who thought she was faking and making excuses for not working. She was also affected by her seeming inability to fulfill the Lord's request. In fact, the Lord had asked Faustian to start several forms of devotions to his Divine Mercy for people who were in need of his love and compassion, people who were afflicted with suffering and guilt as a result of the Second World War. These people must learn to trust completely in the Lord's divine mercy and be merciful to others.

With complete dedication and in union with Jesus, Sister Faustina offered all her prayers, works, and sufferings for those who had lost their faith in God. The Lord also appeared to Faustina in the form of a child so that she could learn the spirituality of humility and trust as in the "little way" of St. Teresa of Lisieux.

Faustina died on October 5, 1938 and her message of Divine Mercy began to spread in Poland and then to all over the world. Her physical death was just the start of a spiritual rebirth. She wrote: "I feel certain that my mission will not come to an end upon my death, but will begin. O doubting souls, I will draw aside for you the veils of heaven to convince you of God's goodness, so that you will no longer continue to wound with your distrust the sweetest Heart of Jesus. God is Love and Mercy" (*Diary*, 281).[31]

In a world torn by conflict and hate, this spiritual healing brought about by the Divine Mercy of Our Lord through Faustina is exactly what we need today. Born almost on the eve of the Second World War, the message

---

30. The information on the life of Faustina Kowalska in this chapter has been adapted from Kosicki and Came, *Faustina, Saint for Our Times*.

31. All references from the *Diary* are taken from Kowalska, *Diary of Saint Maria Faustina Kowalska*.

of divine mercy spread throughout the world. John Paul II wrote: "Her mission continues and is yielding astonishing fruit. It is truly marvelous how her devotion to the merciful Jesus is spreading in our contemporary world and gaining so many human hearts! This is doubtlessly a sign of the times—a sign of our 20th century."[32]

Saintliness and Suffering

Saintliness and sufferings seem inseparable. All saints suffered in one form or another. Like Margaret Alacoque, Helena Kowalska had to suffer many trials, illnesses, misunderstanding, and mistrusts, and finally won acceptance before she died at an early age of thirty-three. Actually within three weeks of entering the convent, Helena wanted to leave. She wanted to enter into a stricter form of life with more time for prayers, but the Lord intervened with a vision of his face in agony when Helena asked, "Jesus, who has hurt you so?" and Jesus replied, "It is you who will cause Me this pain if you leave this convent. It is to this place that I called you and nowhere else, and [it is here] I have prepared many graces for you" (*Diary*, 19).

One of the spiritual trials of Faustina was the temptation to leave her community to found a new congregation. She felt it was Jesus' command that she should start a new institute, but at every turn, she met with resistance. These conflicts and confusions led her to trust the Lord more and more.

Thus, Helena remained with the Sisters of Our Lady of Mercy, received the habit on April 30, 1926, and adopted the religious name Faustina, as mentioned earlier. On that day, she knew her life would not be an easy one, she wrote: "The day I took the [religious] habit, God let me understand how much I was to suffer. I clearly saw to what I was committing myself. I experienced a moment of that suffering. But then God filled my soul again with great consolations" (*Diary*, 22).

Toward the end of her first year in the novitiate, Faustina experienced the kind of suffering which would be part of her life and mission, the experience of the mystic—the dark night of the soul: "darkness began to cast its shadow over my soul. I felt no consolation in prayer; I had to make a great effort to meditate; fear began to sweep over me. Going deeper into myself, I could find nothing but great misery. I could also clearly see the great holiness of God. I did not dare to raise my eyes to Him, but reduced myself to

---

32. John Paul II, "What is Divine Mercy?"

dust under His feet and begged for mercy" (*Diary*, 23). Later, she wrote: "After such sufferings the soul finds itself in a state of great purity of spirit and very close to God. But I should add that during these spiritual torments it is close to God, but it is blind" (*Diary*, 109).

Faustina's response to this dark night of the soul reveals her spirituality and mission in the church: "During these terrible moments I said to God, 'Jesus, who in the Gospel compare Yourself to a most tender mother, I trust in Your words because You are Truth and Life. In spite of everything, Jesus, I trust in You in the face of every interior sentiment which sets itself against hope. Do what You want with me; I will never leave You, because You are the source of my life.'" (*Diary*, 24) Trusting fully in the Lord becomes the hallmark of Faustina's spirituality. Near the end of her novitiate, she had experienced both interior/inner suffering and physical illness. Her yearning and love for God became more intense when she was aware of her own misery. She wrote:

> I am an abyss of misery, and hence I understand that whatever good there is in my soul consists solely of His holy grace. The knowledge of my own misery allows me, at the same time, to know the immensity of Your mercy. In my own interior life, I am looking with one eye at the abyss of my misery and baseness, and with the other, at the abyss of Your mercy, O God. (*Diary*, 56)

Faustina suffered from a spiritual pain like "an internal stigmata":[33] "His Passion was imprinted on my body in an invisible manner, but no less painfully" (*Diary*, 964). She began to learn that suffering, a gift from God, was the road to sanctity: "Suffering is a great grace; through suffering the soul becomes like the Savior; in suffering love becomes crystallized; the greater the suffering, the purer the love" (*Diary*, 57).

After taking her simple vows, Faustina was assigned to a convent in Warsaw where she worked in the kitchen. She fell ill and was sent to the infirmary. Besides this physical ailment, she also had interior struggles. The community was rather harsh towards her and many of the sisters thought she was avoiding work by pretending to be sick. Like Alacoque, Faustina was misunderstood by members of her own community, which obviously pained her most grievously.

Mother Michael, the superior who admitted her into the convent, could see the hand of the Lord in Faustina's suffering: "Sister, along your path, sufferings just spring up out of the ground, I look upon you, Sister,

---

33. Kosicki and Came, *Faustina, Saint for Our Time*, 50.

as one crucified. But I can see that Jesus has a hand in this. Be faithful to the Lord." (*Diary*, 149) In spite of her suffering, Faustina remained steadfast and faithful to her duties as a cook, gardener, or porter, when she was healthy. Although the work was tedious or monotonous, she could see beyond her dull existence with her eyes of faith.

Faustina was a blessing to her superiors because she was obedient and was always ready to take up a new assignment in a different convent whenever there was a need. Throughout the years, she suffered from a chronic tubercular condition due to the demanding work. She was also afflicted by spiritual torment and could not find an appropriate spiritual director. Her fellow sisters found her strange and the gossips of others distressed her greatly. She consulted Jesus, who told her: "Do not fear; I am with you" (*Diary*, 129). Saints and mystics go through periods of physical sufferings and spiritual afflictions in order to attain enlightenment. Their sufferings lead them to greater trust in God. Faustina is no exception—the path to holiness is the narrow road of suffering.

Image of the Divine Mercy

In the midst of Faustina's suffering, the Lord revealed the image of his divine mercy on February 22, 1931. She wrote:

> In the evening, when I was in my cell, I saw the Lord Jesus clothed in a white garment. One hand [was] raised in the gesture of blessing, the other was touching the garment at the breast. From beneath the garment, slightly drawn aside at the breast, there were emanating two large rays, one red, the other pale. In silence I kept my gaze fixed on the Lord; my soul was struck with awe, but also with great joy. After a while, Jesus said to me, Paint an image according to the pattern you see, with the signature: Jesus, I trust in You. I desire that this image be venerated, first in your chapel, and [then] throughout the world. (*Diary*, 47)

Jesus promised her that the person who venerates this image will not be lost or perish. He promised victory over the person's enemies especially at the hour of death. Jesus will defend the person as his own. This was the first major revelation of divine mercy to Faustina, which is very similar to the revelation of the Sacred Heart of Jesus to Margaret Mary Alacoque. Through this revelation to Faustina, Jesus also made known his great desire that all would experience his mercy that comes from his Heart, pierced for us with water and blood flowing: "one of the soldiers pierced his side with a spear, and at once there came out blood and water" (John 19:34). In this image, the two rays, which represent water and blood, issued forth from Jesus' tender mercy. The rays also shield souls from the anger of the Father. Jesus also revealed to Faustina that he desired the Feast of Mercy to be solemnly celebrated on the first Sunday after Easter.

Faustina prayed for a spiritual director who could help her to discern God's will. Her wish was granted when Rev. Michael Sopocko, beatified on September 28, 2008, became her spiritual director. It was Sopocko who helped Faustina by arranging a local artist, Eugene Kazimirowski, to paint the image of Divine Mercy in 1934. It was also Sopocko who had the painting of Divine Mercy displayed at Ostra Brama, the Shrine of Our Lady of Mercy in Vilnius. Sopocko was sensitive to her spiritual development and directed her to keep a diary.[34] Under his spiritual guidance, Faustina grew in wisdom and love and she was able to offer herself for sinners and for those who have lost hope in God's mercy.

Spirituality of St. Faustina

The spirituality of all saints and mystics is this basic union with God although each individual has his or her own special emphasis. In the spirituality of Faustina, the stress is on trust and mercy. Throughout her short life, Faustina displayed tremendous trust in Jesus in spite of all her trials and sufferings. Trusting in Jesus, she revealed to us the infinite mercy of God. A thorough study of the *Diary of St Faustina* reveals this central theme: "Trust in God's Mercy."[35] To trust here means to abandon oneself to the truth of the word of God. The Lord revealed to Faustina these words:

> Let souls who are striving for perfection particularly adore My mercy, because the abundance of graces which I grant them flows from My mercy. I desire that these souls distinguish themselves by boundless trust in My mercy. I myself will attend to the sanctification of such souls. I will provide them with everything they will need to attain sanctity. The graces of My mercy are drawn by means of one vessel only, and that is—trust. The more a soul trusts, the more it will receive. (*Diary*, 1578)

---

34. Ibid., 37–39.
35. Ibid., 73.

Faustina described how she was transformed from a state of great anguish to one of trust in the Lord through submission to God's will (*Diary*, 1498). This trust leads to the experience of the joy of thanksgiving in the presence of the Sacred Heart of Jesus:

> O my Lord, while calling to mind all Your blessings, in the presence of Your Most Sacred Heart, I have felt the need to be particularly grateful for so many graces and blessings from God. I want to plunge myself in thanksgiving before the Majesty of God and to continue in this prayer of thanksgiving for seven days and seven nights; and although I will outwardly carry out all my duties, my spirit will nonetheless stand continually before the Lord, and all my exercises will be imbued with the spirit of thanksgiving. (*Diary*, 1367)

The second feature of Faustina's spirituality is, of course, her focus on divine mercy. John Paul II equates mercy with love: "For mercy is an indispensable dimension of love; it is as it were love's second name and, at the same time, the specific manner in which love is revealed and effected *vis-a-vis* the reality of the evil that is in the world, affecting and besieging man, insinuating itself even into his heart and capable of causing him to 'perish in Gehenna.'"[36]

At the heart of Faustina's vision and inspiration is the certainty that the Lord reveals the mystery of his mercy and that he had chosen her to be the channel of this gift to the world:

> My daughter, know that My Heart is mercy itself. From this sea of mercy, graces flow out upon the whole world. No soul that has approached Me has ever gone away unconsoled. All misery gets buried in the depths of My mercy, and every saving and sanctifying grace flows from this fountain. My daughter, I desire that your heart be an abiding place of My mercy. I desire that this mercy flow out upon the whole world through your heart. Let no one who approaches you go away without that trust in My mercy which I so ardently desire for souls. (*Diary*, 1777)

The world at this present time needs urgently this message of mercy and reconciliation in the midst of so many conflicts and rivalries even among the various Christian churches.

---

36. John Paul II, *Dives in Misericordia*, no. 7.

Call to Christian Unity

Devotion to the Sacred Heart of Jesus developed at the time when there were intense conflict and mistrust between the Catholic Church and the Protestant churches as well as the Eastern churches. Devotion to the Divine Mercy became popular at a time when the Catholic Church attempted and was still attempting to reach out to our separated brethren for the sake of ecclesial unity. In fact, promoting Christian unity is one of the main concerns of the Second Vatican Council. This commitment towards Christian unity is expressed in the Council's *Decree on Ecumenism*. John Paul II repeated this call to unity in his encyclical, *That They May be One* (*Ut Unum Sint*).

In an ecumenical gathering in Paris on May 31, 1980, John Paul II spoke of the "healing and purification of memories." This phrase was an important principle in his efforts to reach out to members of other Christian communities, especially to the Orthodox Church. In his encyclical *Ut Unum Sint*, he teaches that the "commitment to ecumenism must be based upon the conversion of hearts and upon prayer, which will also lead to the *necessary purification of past memories*."[37] John Paul II, referring to the 1965 lifting of Orthodox-Roman Catholic excommunications, notes that such effort removed from our memory and from the church the painful event of the past through "a solemn act which was at once a healing of historical memories, a mutual forgiveness, and a firm commitment to strive for communion."[38] The purification of memory refers to the memory of history.

Further, in 2001, Pope John Paul II in his address to Archbishop Christodoulos of Athens, the primate of the Orthodox Church in Greece, said, "certainly we are burdened by past and present controversies and by enduring misunderstandings. But in a spirit of mutual charity these can and must be overcome, for that is what the Lord asks of us. Clearly there is a need for a liberating process of purification of memory."[39] He admitted that the Catholic Church has sinned against their Orthodox brothers and sisters by their actions and omissions and thus asked the Lord for pardon.

---

37. John Paul II, *Ut unum sint*, no. 2. This material in this section appeared in Mong, *Purification of Memory*, xiii–xvi.

38. John Paul II, *Ut unum sint*, no. 2.

39. John Paul II, "Address of John Paul II to his Beatitude Christodoulos," no. 2.

Referring to the "disastrous sack of the imperial city of Constantinople, which was for so long the bastion of Christianity in the East," John Paul II said, "it is tragic that the assailants, who had set out to secure free access for Christians to the Holy Land, turned against their own brothers in the faith. The fact that they were Latin Christians fills Catholics with deep regret ... Together we must work for this healing if Europe now emerging is to be true to its identity, which is inseparable from the Christian humanism shared by East and West."[40] He also acknowledged that since apostolic times till now, the Orthodox Church of Greece has influenced the Latin Church in its liturgy, spirituality, and jurisprudence. Hence the universal church acknowledges the debt it owes to Greek Christianity especially for the teachings of the Fathers in the East.

Throughout his pontificate, John Paul II always insisted that true ecumenism will not take place without inner conversion and the purification of memory, without holiness and fidelity to the gospel message, and without assiduous prayer that reflects the prayer of Jesus. Inner conversion implies that the church admits the wrongs and atrocities it has done in the past and seeks forgiveness from God and also from the victims. Georges Cottier says, "The forgiveness of God is precisely the highest and most eminent form of the purification of memory. This is because the divine forgiveness really erases and destroys the sin, so that its weight does not burden the conscience anymore."[41] It is essential that the church must be purified not only of the faults it has inflicted on others, but of the memory of the violence and persecutions it has suffered in the past.

This healing of memory is needed for the church's integrity of mission, and is also required as part of the ecumenical effort to dialogue. In practice, this healing of memories can be done through four fundamental methods: spiritual-psychological, academic, liturgical, and human service. Through dialogue, we make an effort not to allow our memories to dwell on the sins and wrongs we have committed but to focus on what we have in common. Recommended by the The Roman Catholic-Mennonite Dialogue, it states: ". . . although we are not in full unity with one another, the substantial amount of the Apostolic faith which we realize today that we share, allows us as members of the Catholic and Mennonite delegations to see one another as brothers and sisters in Christ."[42]

40. Ibid.
41. Cottier, "The purification of memory," 259.
42. "Called Together to Be Peacemakers," no. 210.

This statement can also be applied to members of the other Christian churches. In this document, John Paul II also stressed the need for theological dialogue that can help in the healing of memories by assisting the dialogue partners to discover to what extent they continue to share the Christian faith in spite of centuries of division. They can explain their tradition to one another, which will lead to a deeper mutual understanding and a deeper realization that they hold in common many aspects of their Christian heritage.[43]

Eastern Tradition

It is not surprising that the two Polish saints, Pope John Paul II and Sister Faustina, had a special concern and love for Poland. Faustina wrote: "As I was praying for Poland, I heard the words: I bear a special love for Poland, and if she will be obedient to My will, I will exalt her in might and holiness. From her will come forth the spark that will prepare the world for My final coming." (*Diary*, 1732)

The Polish Church occupies a very special place in Christianity with its unique blend of oriental and occidental spirituality because of its geographical location, serving as the crossroad between Eastern and Western Europe. St. Cyril and his brother, St. Methodius, brought the Christian faith from Constantinople to Moravia and southwestern Poland during the ninth century. Thus, Pope John Paul II speaks of the rich treasures that are part of the Eastern Church in *Orientale Lumen*. He implores the divine mercy for unity between the East and the West: "And if sometimes, in their [Western Churches] relations with the Orthodox Churches, misunderstandings and open opposition have arisen, we all know that we must ceaselessly implore divine mercy and a new heart capable of reconciliation over and above any wrong suffered or inflicted."[44]

John Paul II considers Faustina "the great apostle of Divine Mercy in our time."[45] It is this divine mercy that may lead to a union of the Eastern and Western Churches. Her life helps to "unlock the mysteries" of both Eastern and Western Spirituality.[46] Faustina successfully integrated the riches of Eastern spirituality into her religious life in her devotion to the

---

43. Ibid., no. 207.
44. John Paul II, *Orientale Lumen*, 21.
45. John Paul II, "What is Divine Mercy?," no. 3.
46. Kosicki and Came, *Faustina, Saint for Our Time*, 86.

sacred liturgy, especially the Eucharist. She was also drawn towards the Trinity and had described her experience of divinization: "I saw the joy of the Incarnate Word, and I was immersed in the Divine Trinity. When I came to myself, longing filled my soul, and I yearned to be united with God." (*Diary*, 1121)

Veneration of icons is an ancient tradition in the Eastern Church. In the icons, the importance of the eyes of Jesus gazing lovingly towards those who look up to him is demonstrated in both the Sacred Heart and Divine Mercy images. The Byzantine fathers focus on gazing and icons are painted for the purpose of helping the faithful who contemplate before the images to enter more profoundly into prayer. The icon speaks gradually to our inner sense, which is our heart. In Poland, the veneration of the icon of Our Lady of Czestochowa is immensely popular. Faustina used to spend hours in prayer before this image of Czestochowa. The image of Divine Mercy, though painted in Western style, "does portray the essence of icons, namely, that of light coming out of darkness and a portrayal of the Passion, Death, and Resurrection of Jesus."[47]

Monasticism is also another revered tradition in the East that spread to the West in various forms. Monastic life had its origin in the desert life of the East. According to John Paul II, "Monasticism has always been the very soul of the Eastern Churches: the first Christian monks were born in the East and the monastic life was an integral part of the Eastern lumen passed on to the West by the great Fathers of the undivided Church."[48] Monasticism has served as a bridge between the East and the West since both Churches have its various forms of "desert life." Faustina had lived this monastic life to the full—she loved the cloistered life and even thought of founding a new institute with more rigorous rules.

Spreading of the Divine Mercy Devotion

Faustina's mission began after her death as devotion to divine mercy spread rapidly throughout Poland. Her grave in Lagiewniki, Cracow, was constantly visited by the faithful from all walks of life, seeking her intercessions. Visitors also came to pray before the Image in the convent chapel on the side altar of the Sacred Heart.

---

47. Ibid., 87.
48. John Paul II, *Orientale Lumen*, no. 9.

The practice spread rapidly because it answered to a felt need of the time. Since the start of World War II in 1939, devotion to the Divine Mercy had become a source of hope and strength for many inmates in concentration camps throughout Poland and beyond. Soldiers and refugees carried the images in many parts of the world such as France, the United States, and Australia. Religious leaders such as the Pallotine and Marian priests became the chief promoters of the Divine Mercy Devotion. Many of their members have received special graces.[49]

Like the Sacred Heart Devotion, Divine Mercy was not at first approved by the Church. In fact, Devotion to Divine Mercy was prohibited with a Notification dated March 6, 1959. Images of the Devotion were removed from churches and Fr. Sopocko himself was admonished by the Holy See for promoting this piety. As a result, novenas, devotions, and images of the Divine Mercy were withdrawn from many churches. It survived only in a small community in Cracow, where Faustina was buried.

In 1963, Cardinal Ottaviani, Prefect of Office, asked Archbishop Karol Wojtyla to promote the cause of beatification of Sister Faustina. He was to act quickly before all the witnesses died. Thus, twenty-seven years after her death, on October 21, 1965, Faustina was given the title "Servant of God" and on January 31, 1968, she was beatified. Cardinal Karol Wojtyla, Archbishop of Cracow, lifted the ban on the Divine Mercy, and six months later, on October 16, 1978, he became Pope John Paul II. In 2000, John Paul II canonized Faustina.

Two Devotions: One Heart

The message of the Sacred Heart first came during the time when the church had to deal with Jansenism, a counter-reform movement influenced by Calvinism. Catholics persecuted the Huguenots, the principal Protestant group in France. In fact, Alacoque had prayed for the conversion of the Huguenots whom she considered as heretics. Thus, devotion to the Sacred Heart of Jesus was promoted vigorously by the Church as an antidote against the spread of Protestantism and for the renewal of Catholic piety. The message of love and mercy propagated by the devotion to the Sacred Heart of Jesus was also urgently needed when France had to address the effects and needs that were associated with the aftermath of violent revolutions in the eighteenth and nineteenth centuries.

49. Michalenko, *The Life of Faustina Kowalska*, 275.

Today, the church faces new challenges and has to deal with secularism and materialism. Many who had suffered from the two world wars desperately needed to forgive and to receive forgiveness. Only the Divine Mercy of Christ can bring about a genuine reconciliation.

The late Pope John Paul II, in his homily at Faustina's Canonization Mass in 2000, preached: "By divine Providence, the life of this humble daughter of Poland was completely linked with the history of the 20th century, the century we have just left behind. In fact, it was between the First and Second World Wars that Christ entrusted his message of mercy to her. Those who remember, who were witnesses and participants in the events of those years and the horrible sufferings they caused for millions of people, know well how necessary was the message of mercy."[50] John Paul II spoke of the necessity of the message of mercy for those who were witnesses and participants in those horrible years of sufferings that affected millions of people. In the midst of the two world wars, God has revealed his grace and mercy, to heal humanity's anger and pain.

The Second Vatican Council promotes Christian unity in its decree on ecumenism. In her own way, Faustina, with her message of Divine Mercy, paved the way for reconciliation between the Eastern and Western churches. She is a symbol of that unity between the two traditions. Faustina was able to integrate the treasures of the oriental church such as her devotion to the sacred liturgy, her love of the Blessed Sacrament, and the Holy Trinity in her religious life.

The image of the Divine Mercy that was revealed to St. Faustina is an icon which appeals to the hearts of the faithful, especially refugees and prisoners. Devotion to Divine Mercy has replaced the Devotion to the Sacred Heart in many places, but it is the same heart of Jesus. Although the form and emphasis is different, the message remains the same—to make known the love and mercy of the Father through his Son, Jesus Christ.

---

50. John Paul II, *Homily of the Holy Father.*

Epilogue

Acts of faith performed publicly are like the Acts of the Apostles: they are inspired by devotion and hope for things unseen in the afterlife. And like the Acts of the Apostles, they can lead to revolutionary change and social upheaval in the here and now. Fishermen, farmers, carpenters, tent makers, and all other poor common folks, whether in the first century or the twenty-first century, have the same yearning for liberation from oppression and poverty. Faith and pious practices are their public expression of hope for a better tomorrow. They may not understand the niceties of church edicts and dogmas but they know in their hearts what is just and free, and that such yearnings are spiritual and come from the heavenly Father who sees all and wants his children to live in peace and plenty.

This work starts off with the assumption that popular piety is a powerful tool for evangelization. Conversely, popular religion can also be a political tool that the dominant class in society manipulates to maintain their status quo. However, popular piety, when guided by enlightened pastors and church authorities emphasizing the liberating message of the gospel, can deepen the spiritual life of the faithful and raise their social and political awareness. It is thus related to the theology of liberation with its stress on the preferential option for the poor, as we have discussed in chapter 1.

Latin American nations and the Philippines share many common characteristics. Colonized by Spain in sixteenth century, they are predominantly Catholic nations where the majority of the population is still poor, marginalized, and dispossessed. Chapter 2 studied the apparition of Our Lady of Guadalupe in Mexico and its significance, and in chapter 3, we explored the various devotional practices in the Philippines, namely, devotions to Santo Niño of Cebu, the suffering Christ, and Our Lady of Perpetual Help.

Chapter 4 discussed the issue of culture in popular piety and the Church's attempts at accommodation and inculturation to make to faith more relevant and meaningful to the faithful. A good example of accommodation and inculturation is the efforts made by Matteo Ricci (1552–1610) in China. The Church has looked upon popular piety as a treasure of the faithful but insists that these devotions must be in harmony with its official liturgy.

Chapter 5 discussed some of the important issues in the Church document the *Directory on Popular Piety and the Liturgy*, underscoring the possible conflict between Church worship and popular religious practices. This chapter examined the fine line between superstition and piety with reference to the Chinese cult of ancestor veneration.

In chapter 6, we studied specifically the devotional practices of Hong Kong Catholics, focusing on the significance of Our Lady of Medjugorje. Many people who have visited Medjugorje have experienced peace and conversion in their personal lives. Chapter 7 examined how devotion to the Sacred Heart of Jesus had gradually been replaced by devotion to the Divine Mercy, which is celebrated by with great enthusiasm by the local Catholics here. Divine Mercy has great appeal because its message is relevant to a society afflicted by family problems, failed relationships, and breakdown in marriages.

In conclusion, we reflected on the popularity of pilgrimages among Hong Kong Catholics, where such spiritual tours are organized throughout the year. For example, Rev. Paulus Santoso, an Indonesian Carmelite priest working in Hong Kong, accompanied forty-six pilgrims to the Holy Land as their spiritual director in May 2018. He was assisted by Stanislaus Lee, a biblical scholar who is well-versed in Jewish culture and customs. They visited the sites of Jesus' life and ministry as portrayed in the New Testament, such as Galilee, Bethany, the Mount of Beatitude, and Jerusalem. Santoso said he was deeply impressed during his journey to the Mount Calvary where Jesus was crucified. Celebrating the Eucharist with the Hong Kong pilgrims in Cantonese in a small chapel near the tomb of Jesus was the high point of his visit.

Pilgrims are usually deeply touched by their visits to the most sacred sites of Christianity. Perhaps this is one of the reasons why pilgrimages are so popular, especially in Hong Kong, among Christians who want to go on a spiritual quest instead of treading the usual tourist path. These journeys

Epilogue

in search for the sacred offer Hong Kongers opportunities to see, touch, smell, and feel the places connected with their faith.

Richard R. Niebuhr captures the essence of pilgrimage well: "Pilgrims are persons in motion—passing through territories not their own—seeking something we might call completion . . . These physical passings through apertures can print themselves deeply into us, not in our physical senses alone but in our spiritual sense as well, so that what we apprehend outwardly becomes part of the lasting geography of our souls."[1]

One of the oldest physical and spiritual exercises in Christianity, the pilgrimage occurs in other religious traditions as well. It can simply be described as going on a journey to a sacred place to request a favor or as an act of penance either individually or as a group. For most people, it is an opportunity to renew their faith and to be acquainted with the history, geography, and the spirit of their religion. Some go on a pilgrimage in search of physical or spiritual healing, such as travelling to Lourdes. Many return from pilgrimages with new hope and inspiration. Often, the experience is so profound that they cannot express it in words alone. The journey itself is as important as the experience of the sacredness of the sites.

Hindus journey to bathe at the sacred river of Ganges, for example, during the Kumbh Mela festival that occurs every twelve years. This mega festival attracts more than fifty million visitors who purify themselves by bathing at the confluence of the Ganges and Yamuna rivers with the hope of breaking the cycle of reincarnation. Jews read about the journeys of Abraham, Moses, and Joseph in the Old Testament. Muslims travel to Mecca to complete a pilgrimage called the *Hajj*, a compulsory religious duty that must be carried out at least once in their lifetime. In fact, Muslims believe Abraham and his son Ishmael were the first pilgrims.

In Catholicism, the pilgrimage has always been an important tradition. In Western Europe, the earliest shrines and places of pilgrimage were the catacombs (cemeteries) of early Christian martyrs buried outside the walls of Roman cities. Pilgrims started visiting the tombs of the martyrs as a form of devotion. In fact, Christians tried to arrange burial places for their loved ones close to the martyrs' tombs because they believed the sites were sacred, and thus close to heaven in a mystical way. Pilgrimages to the Holy Land also started very early in the church when Christianity was legalized by Emperor Constantine in the fourth century.

---

1. Quoted in Clift and Clift, *The Archetype of Pilgrimage*, 1–2.

Rituals are very important in Catholicism. At the sacred shrine or church, pilgrims may take part in procession, pray the rosary, confess their sins, and participate in the Eucharist. While most pilgrims practice the same in their home parishes, performing the spiritual exercises in these sacred places in a foreign land has a special meaning for them. Some people believe that miracles and apparitions of the Virgin would occur again at the sites of pilgrimage.

In most pilgrimages, there is the prevalence of superstitious beliefs, such as beliefs in the power of relics, holy water, and images. Thus the church's attitude is rather ambivalent towards such devotion. This clearly is the case regarding the Vatican's position towards the apparitions at Medjugorje. Being aware that vestiges of magic and superstitious beliefs still linger in advanced religions as well, the church rightly calls for caution and prudence.

There is one non-Marian sanctuary that is quite well-known in the literary world, the Shrine of St. Thomas Becket at Canterbury, one of the most famous pilgrim sites in late medieval Europe. Becket defended the rights of the Church against the interference of King Henry II and was assassinated in his own cathedral in 1270. In *The Canterbury Tales*, published in 1476, Geoffrey Chaucer used the pilgrimage to the Shrine of St. Thomas Becket as a framing device where individual characters began to tell their stories.

Since the Middle Ages, majority of the Catholic pilgrimages have been to Marian Shrines. In the Philippines, pilgrimages to the shrines in Antipolo, Manaog, and Baclaran are very popular. In Pakistan, the National Marian shrine at Mariamabad attracts both Christian and Muslim visitors. In Vietnam, the Marian shrine at La Vang is well known among Catholics and non-Catholics. The shrine of Sheshan near Shanghai has been visited by pilgrims not only from mainland China, but also from Taiwan and Hong Kong.

Marian apparitions have a few things in common. The Virgin Mary pleads for repentance, penance, and prayer with a promise of protection and healing of the sick and the broken hearted. She remains an intercessor between God and us. As the mother of God, she wields great influence over God's judgments. She pacifies God's wrath on our behalf as Mother of Mercy. Mary's powerful intercession is seen in sharp contrast to our human sinfulness and hopelessness. This was demonstrated in Mary's request for repentance during her apparitions at Lourdes in 1858 and at Fatima in 1917 with its apocalyptic visions and warnings.

Epilogue

In contrast to the terrifying apocalyptic message of Fatima, the apparition of the Virgin of Guadalupe portrayed God as warm and compassionate. As we have seen, the origin of Mexican Christianity has its roots in the devotion to Our Lady of Guadalupe. She has become the powerful symbol of social and political liberation for the people of Mexico and also for the other nations in Latin America.

Marian apparitions are usually seen by poor and simple folk. The relationship between popular piety and the poor is thus of great significance. Latin American theologians have reflected on how the poor's religious experience have been influenced and shaped by poverty, injustice, and exploitation. This religious experience can be liberating or alienating; it depends to a large extent on the leadership in the church: do they make the effort to conscientize the poor regarding the injustice and inequality that are prevalent in society or are they only concerned about maintaining the status quo of the establishment?

Popular piety such as devotion to the Blessed Virgin Mary can be excessive and idolatrous if not checked and directed by ecclesiastical authorities. Some of these excesses are the result of poor catechizing or evangelizing. Perhaps the liturgical celebrations fail to satisfy the spiritual needs of the faithful. The paschal mystery, which stands at the heart of Christianity, must become a transforming reality in the lives of the faithful; it must not be just an intellectual assent to a set of doctrines.

Be that as it may, popular religion is here to stay, especially in Asia, among Christians and non-Christians. I would like to end this epilogue with a reflection by a young Singaporean regarding the newly renovated Novena Church, opened in 2017, a Marian shrine dedicated to Our Lady of Perpetual Succor. Andre Joseph Theng writes:

> Perhaps it is the competitive, consumeristic fast-paced lifestyle that forces its citizens to seek some kind of spirituality or peace, no matter how temporary. More likely, in my own opinion, with the vast majority of Singaporeans influenced by Chinese religion, and combined with the pragmatic nature of Singapore society, the relationship between the Singaporean and the deity can be described as one of pragmatic. In this sense, it is perhaps not surprising that the image of "Our Lady of Perpetual Succor" has become the favorite Catholic icon in Singapore, one where people can ask for favors to be granted, where one can bring their dreams and desires to.

Power of Popular Piety

Established in 1948, the Church of St. Alphonsus in Singapore, commonly known as Novena Church, grew rapidly as thousands of Catholics and non-Catholics came to petition and to give thanks to the Blessed Virgin Mary during the Saturday novenas. Soon the district became known as Novena and when the Mass Transit Rail was introduced, the station was given the name Novena Station. Seventy years since the church celebrated its first mass, people from all walks of life, Christians, Buddhists, Taoists, Muslims, and even those without religion, continue to flock to the Shrine of Our Lady of Perpetual Succor at 300 Thomson Road, Singapore, to seek her help and consolation. Such is the power of popular piety—it transcends religious, cultural, social, and political barriers.

Bibliography

Abeyasingha, Nihal. "Popular piety and liturgy." *Pastoral Life* 51 (November 2002) 21–26.
Anderson, Carl, and Eduardo Chávez. *Our Lady of Guadalupe: Mother of the Civilization of Love*. New York: Image, 2009.
Andrić, Ivo. *The Bridge Over The Drina*. London: The Harvill, 1995.
Anon. "Called together to be peacemakers: The International Dialogue between the Catholic Church and the Mennonite World Conference, 1998–2003." *One in Christ* 39, no. 3 (July 2004) 80–142.
Aquinas, Thomas. *The Summa Theologica* (1947). https://dhspriory.org/thomas/summa/.
The Aswang Project. https://www.aswangproject.com/bathala/.
Auer, Johann. "Devotion to the Sacred Heart and the Theology of Conversion." In *Faith in Christ and the Worship of Christ: New Approaches to Devotion to Christ*, edited by Leo Scheffczyk, translated by Graham Harrison, 119–140. San Francisco: Ignatius, 1986.
"Aztec." *Encyclopedia Britannica*. https://www.britannica.com/topic/Aztec.
Baier, Walter. "Key Issues in Medieval Sacred Heart Piety." In *Faith in Christ and the Worship of Christ: New Approaches to Devotion to Christ*, edited by Leo Scheffczyk, translated by Graham Harrison, 81–99. San Francisco: Ignatius, 1986.
Bastian, Jean Pierre. "Popular religion: a strategic element for the formation of a new hegemonic block in Latin America." *Foundations* 23, no. 4 (October 1980) 355–67.
"Bathala, the Tagalog God." *Tagalog Lang*. https://www.tagaloglang.com/bathala-the-tagalog-god/.
Bautista, Julius. "The Rebellion and the Icon: Holy Revolutions in the Philippines." *Asian Journal of Social Science* 34, no. 2 (2006) 291–310.
Bax, Mart. "The Madonna of Medjugorje: Religious Rivalry and the Formation of a Devotional Movement in Yugoslavia." *Anthropological Quarterly* 63, no. 2 (1990) 63–75.
Becker, Joachim SS, CC. "The Heart in the Language of the Bible." In *Faith in Christ and the Worship of Christ: New Approaches to Devotion to Christ*, edited by Leo Scheffczyk, translated by Graham Harrison, 23–31. San Francisco: Ignatius, 1986.
Benedict XVI, Pope. "Benedict XVI, Pope (2011-04-08) Popular piety and the new evangelization." *L'osservatore Romano* 2190 (April 13, 2011) 4.
Berryman, Edward. "Medjugorje's living icons: making spirit matter (for sociology)." *Social Compass* 48, no. 4 (2001) 593–610.
Boff, Leonardo. *Church: Charism and Power—Liberation Theology and the Institutional Church*. London: SCM, 1984.

Bibliography

———. "Toward a Christology of Liberation" (1972). In *Liberation Theology: A Documentary History*, edited by Alfred T. Hennelly, 159–62. Maryknoll, NY: Orbis, 1990.

Bonino, José Míguez. "Popular Piety in Latin America." In *The Mystical and Political Dimension of the Christian Faith*, edited by Claude Geffré and Gustavo Gutiérrez, 148–57. New York: Herder and Herder, 1974.

Brading, D. A. *Mexican Phoenix: Our Lady of Guadalupe: Image and Tradition Across Five Centuries*. Cambridge: Cambridge University Press, 2001.

Brockey, Liam Matthew. *Journey to the East the Jesuit Mission to China, 1579–1724*. Cambridge, MA: Belknap Press of Harvard University Press, 2008.

Brundage, Burr C. *A Rain of Darts: The Mexican Aztecs*. Austin, TX: University of Texas Press, 1972.

Callahan, Annice, RSCJ. *Karl Rahner's Spirituality of the Pierced Heart: A Reinterpretation of the Devotion to the Sacred Heart*. Lanham, MD: University Press of America, 1985.

"Called Together to Be Peacemakers—Report of the International Dialogue between the Catholic Church and Mennonite World Conference 1998–2003." (August 2003.) http://www.vatican.va/roman_curia/pontifical_councils/chrstuni/mennonite-conference-docs/rc_pc_chrstuni_doc_20110324_mennonite_en.html.

Candelaria, Michael R. *Popular Religion and Liberation: The Dilemma of Liberation Theology*. SUNY Series in Religion, Culture, and Society. Albany, NY: State University of New York Press, 1990.

Carroll, Warren H. *Our Lady of Guadalupe and the Conquest of Darkness*. Front Royal, VA: Christendom, 1983.

Catechism of the Catholic Church. http://www.vatican.va/archive/ccc_css/archive/catechism/p2s2c4a1.htm.

Catholic Culture. The Revelation of the Sacred Heart of Jesus Paral-le-Monial, France. https://www.catholicculture.org/culture/library/view.cfm?recnum=5796.

Cebulski, Jan. "Medjugorje—hallucination or truth." *Religion in Communist Dominated Areas* 23, nos. 10–12 (1984) 143–44.

Chadwick, Owen. *The Secularization of the European Mind in the Nineteenth Century: The Gifford Lectures in the University of Edinburgh for 1973–4*. Gifford Lectures, 1973–1974. Cambridge: Cambridge University Press, 1975.

Chan, Chung-Yan Joyce. "Commands from heaven: Matteo Ricci's Christianity in the eyes of Ming Confucian officials." *Missiology* 31, no. 3 (July 2003) 269–87.

Chien, Teresa. "A Catholic View on Ancestor Remembrance and related issues." New Taipei: Research Centre for Liturgy, Fu Jen Faculty of Theology of St. Robert Bellarmine, 2002. http://theology.catholic.org.tw/public/liyi/topics_ancestor.html.

"Christian Catacombs, The." http://www.vatican.va/roman_curia/pontifical_commissions/archeo/inglese/documents/rc_com_archeo_doc_20011010_cataccrist_en.html.

Chung, Paul S. "Christian-Confucian dialogue in construction of cultural reality: global-critical, intercivilizational, and postcolonial." *Ching Feng* 11, no. 1 (2012) 55–78.

———. "Inculturation and the recognition of the other: Matteo Ricci's legacy in the Christian-Confucian context." *Studies in Interreligious Dialogue* 20, no. 1 (2010) 79–97.

Chupungco, Anscar J. *Cultural Adaptation of the Liturgy*. Mahwah, NJ: Paulist, 1982.

———. *Liturgical Inculturation: Sacramentals, Religiosity, and Catechesis*. Collegeville, MN: Liturgical, 1992.

———. *Liturgies of the Future: The Process and Methods of Inculturation.* New York: Paulist, 1989.
Clift, Jean Dalby, and Wallace B. Clift. *The Archetype of Pilgrimage: Outer Action with Inner Meaning. Jung and Spirituality.* New York: Paulist, 1996.
Climenhaga, Alison Fitchett. "The Huei tlamahuiçoltica: Responding to Pastoral Challenges in Light of Our Lady of Guadalupe." In *New Frontiers in Guadalupan Studies,* edited by Virgilio Elizondo and Timothy Matovina, 65–87. Eugene, OR: Pickwick, 2014.
Congregation for Divine Worship and the Discipline of the Sacraments. *Directory on Popular Piety and the Liturgy: Principles and Guidelines* (December 2001). www.vatican.va/roman_curia/congregations/ccdds/documents/rc_con_ccdds_doc_20020513_vers-direttorio_en.html.
Cottier, Georges Cardinal. "The purification of memory." *Nova Et Vetera* 2, no. 2 (September 2004) 257–66.
Cox, Harvey Gallagher. *The Seduction of the Spirit: The Use and Misuse of People's Religion.* New York: Simon and Schuster, 1973.
Coyle, Kathleen. "Pilgrimages, apparitions and popular piety." *East Asian Pastoral Review* 38, no. 2 (2001) 173–89.
DeVille, Adam A. J. "On the Healing of Memories: An Analysis of the Concept in Papal Documents." http://www.koed.hu/sw249/adam.pdf.
Dingayan, Luna. "Popular Religion and Evangelization: A Philippine Experience." *International Review of Mission* 82, no. 327 (1993) 355–63.
Doyle, Dennis M. "The Concept of Inculturation in Roman Catholicism: A Theological Consideration." *U.S. Catholic Historian* 30, no. 1 (2012) 1–13.
Dunne, George H. *Generation of Giants: The Story of the Jesuits in China in the Last Decades of the Ming Dynasty.* Notre Dame, IN: University of Notre Dame Press, 1962.
Dussel, Enrique D. *Philosophy of Liberation.* Maryknoll, NY: Orbis, 1985.
Dyrness, William A. *Invitation to Cross-cultural Theology: Case Studies in Vernacular Theologies.* Grand Rapids: Zondervan, 1992.
Eagleson, John, and Philip J. Scharper, eds. *Conferencia General Del Episcopado Latinoamericano. Puebla and Beyond: Documentation and Commentary.* Maryknoll, NY: Orbis, 1979.
Elders, Leo, SVD. "The Inner Life of Jesus in the Theology and Devotion of Saint Thomas Aquinas." In *Faith in Christ and the Worship of Christ: New Approaches to Devotion to Christ,* edited by Leo Scheffczyk, translated by Graham Harrison, 65–79. San Francisco: Ignatius, 1986.
Elizondo, Virgilio. "Evangelization Is Inculturation: A Case Study." *Missiology: An International Review* 43, no. 1 (2015) 17–26.
Elizondo, Virgilio P., and Timothy Matovina. *New Frontiers in Guadalupan Studies.* Eugene, OR: Pickwick, 2014.
Emmons, D. D. "Devotion to the Sacred Heart: How did this popular Catholic practice come about?" *Our Sunday Visitor* (January 30, 2009). https://www.osv.com/OSVNewsweekly/Story/TabId/2672/ArtMID/13567/ArticleID/2560/Devotion-to-the-Sacred-Heart.aspx.
Erasmus. *The Enchiridion of Erasmus.* Translated and edited by Raymond Himelick. Bloomington, IN: Indiana University Press, 1963.
Fitchett, Climenhaga Alison. "The Huei tlamahuiçoltica: Responding to Pastoral Challenges in Light of Our Lady of Guadalupe." In *New Frontiers in Guadalupan*

Studies, edited by Virgilio Elizondo and Timothy Matovina, 65–87. Eugene, OR: Pickwick, 2014.

Fontana, Michela. *Matteo Ricci: A Jesuit in the Ming Court.* Lanham, MD: Rowman & Littlefield, 2011.

Francis, Pope. "Homily on popular piety." *Originsonline.Com* 43, no. 2 (May 16, 2013) 29–31.

———. *Holy Mass on the Occasion of the Day of Confraternities* (May 5, 2013). http://w2.vatican.va/content/francesco/en/homilies/2013/documents/papa-francesco_20130505_omelia-confraternite.html.

Freire, Paulo. "'Conscientisation'." *Cross Currents* 24, no. 1 (1974) 23–31.

———. "Conscientizing as a Way of Liberating" (1970). In *Liberation Theology: A Documentary History*, edited by Alfred T. Hennelly, 5–13. Maryknoll, NY: Orbis, 1990.

Galilea, Segundo. "The Theology of Liberation and the Place of 'Folk Religion'." In *What Is Religion?: An Inquiry for Christian Theology*, edited by Mircea Eliade, David Tracy, and Marcus Lefébure, 40–45. *Concilium* 136. Edinburgh: New York: T. & T. Clark, 1980.

Gener, Timoteo. "The Catholic Imagination and Popular Religion in Lowland Philippines: Missiological Significance of David Tracy's Theory of Religious Imaginations." *Mission Studies* 22, no. 1 (2005) 25–57.

Gittins, Anthony J. "Faith, piety and non-institutional Christianity: popular religion among homeless women." *New Theology Review* 13 (May 2000) 38–48.

Górny, Grzegorz, and Janusz Rosikon. *Guadalupe Mysteries: Deciphering the Code.* San Francisco: Ignatius, 2016.

Greeley, Andrew M. *The Catholic Imagination.* Berkeley, CA: University of California Press, 2000.

Gruenwald, Oskar. "The Bridge to Eternity: Medjugorje and the Yugoslav Civil War." *Journal of Interdisciplinary Studies* 8, nos. 1–2 (1996) 131–48.

Guan Yin. *New World Encyclopaedia.* http://www.newworldencyclopedia.org/entry/Guan_Yin.

Gutiérrez, Gustavo. *A Theology of Liberation: History, Politics, and Salvation.* Maryknoll, NY: Orbis, 1988.

———. *The Power of the Poor in History: Selected Writings.* London: SCM, 1983.

———. "Towards a Theology of Liberation" (July 1968). In *Liberation Theology: A Documentary History*, edited by Alfred T. Hennelly, 62–76. Maryknoll, NY: Orbis, 1990.

Hart, Roger. *Imagined Civilizations: China, the West, and Their First Encounter.* Baltimore: Johns Hopkins University Press, 2013.

Hebblethwaite, Peter. *The Christian-Marxist Dialogue: Beginnings, Present Status, and beyond—An Exploration Book.* New York: Paulist, 1977.

Heer, Josef. "The Soteriological Significance of the Johannine Image of the Pierced Savior." In *Faith in Christ and the Worship of Christ: New Approaches to Devotion to Christ*, edited by Leo Scheffczyk, translated by Graham Harrison, 33–46. San Francisco: Ignatius, 1986.

Hennelly, Alfred T. *Liberation Theology: A Documentary History.* Maryknoll, NY: Orbis, 1990.

Herrero, Juan A. "Medjugorje: ecclesiastical conflict, theological controversy, ethnic division." *Research in the Social Scientific Study of Religion* 10 (1999) 137–70.

Bibliography

Hsia, R. Po-chia. *A Jesuit in the Forbidden City: Matteo Ricci 1552–1610*. Oxford: Oxford University Press, 2010.

Hunt, Robert A. *The Gospel among the Nations : A Documentary History of Inculturation*. American Society of Missiology Series No. 46. Maryknoll, NY: Orbis, 2010.

———. *The Gospel Among the Nations: A Documentary History of Inculturation*. Maryknoll, NY: Orbis, 1976.

Hutchison, William R. *Errand to the World: American Protestant Thought and Foreign Missions*. Chicago: The University of Chicago Press, 1987.

Jay, Martin. *Adorno*. Cambridge, MA: Harvard University Press, 1984.

John Paul II, Pope. Address of John Paul II to his Beatitude Christodoulos, Archbishop of Athens and Primate of Greece. https://w2.vatican.va/content/john-paul-ii/en/speeches/2001/may/documents/hf_jp-ii_spe_20010504_archbishop-athens.html., no.2.

———. *Canonization of Juan Diego Cuauhtlatoatzin*. http://w2.vatican.va/content/john-paul-ii/en/homilies/2002/documents/hf_jp-ii_hom_20020731_canonization-mexico.html.

———. *Dives in Misericordia*. http://w2.vatican.va/content/john-paul-ii/en/encyclicals/documents/hf_jp-ii_enc_30111980_dives-in-misericordia.html.

———. *Ecclesia in America*. http://w2.vatican.va/content/john-paul-ii/en/apost_exhortations/documents/hf_jp-ii_exh_22011999_ecclesia-in-america.html.

———. *Homily of the Holy Father, Mass in St Peter's Square's for the Canonization of Sr. Mary Faustina Kowalska* (April 30, 2000). http://w2.vatican.va/content/john-paul-ii/en/homilies/2000/documents/hf_jp-ii_hom_20000430_faustina.html.

———. *Message of His Holiness Pope John Paul II for the Fourth Centenary of the arrival in Beijing of the great missionary and scientist Matteo Ricci, S.I.* (October 2001). http://w2.vatican.va/content/john-paulii/en/speeches/2001/october/documents/hf_jp-ii_spe_20011024_matteo-ricci.html

———. *Orientale Lumen*. https://w2.vatican.va/content/john-paul-ii/en/apost_letters/1995/documents/hf_jp-ii_apl_19950502_orientale-lumen.html.

———. *Redemptoris Missio: On the permanent validity of the Church's missionary mandate*. http://w2.vatican.va/content/john-paul-ii/en/encyclicals/documents/hf_jp-ii_enc_07121990_redemptoris-missio.html.

———. *Ut unum sint: On commitment to Ecumenism*. http://w2.vatican.va/content/john-paul-ii/en/encyclicals/documents/hf_jp-ii_enc_25051995_ut-unum-sint.html.

———. "What is Divine Mercy?" *The Divine Mercy*. https://www.thedivinemercy.org/message/johnpaul/homilies.php.

Jonas, Raymond. *France and the Cult of the Sacred Heart: An Epic Tale for Modern Times*. Berkeley, CA: University of California Press, 2000.

Kosicki, George W., CSB, and David C. Came. *Faustina, Saint for Our Times: A Personal Look at Her Life, Spirituality, and Legacy*. Stockbridge, MA: Marian, 2015.

Kowalska, Faustina. *Diary of Saint Maria Faustina Kowalska: Divine Mercy in My Soul*. Stockbridge, MA: Marian, 2004.

Küng, Hans, and Julia Ching. *Christianity and Chinese Religions*. London: SCM, 1989.

Lafaye, Jacques. *Quetzalcóatl and Guadalupe: The Formation of Mexican National Consciousness 1531–1813*. Translated by Benjamin Keen. Chicago: University of Chicago Press, 1976.

Bibliography

Lee, Yongho Francis. "Our Lady of Guadalupe in Bernardino de Sahagún's Historia general de las cosas de Nueva España." In *New Frontiers in Guadalupan Studies,* edited by Virgilio Elizondo and Timothy Matovina, 1–18. Eugene, OR: Pickwick, 2014.

Lenin, Vladimir Il'ich. *What Is to Be Done?: Burning Questions of Our Movement.* 1st ed. Peking: Foreign Languages, 1973.

Leon-Portilla, Miguel, ed. *The Broken Spear: The Aztec Account of the Conquest of Mexico.* Boston: Bean, 1962.

Li, Kit-Man, Ka Hing Cheung, and Kun-Sun Chan. "Hong Kong: Catholicism Among the Laity." In *Popular Catholicism in a World Church: Seven Case Studies in Inculturation,* 215–248. Maryknoll, NY: Orbis, 1999.

Li, Zhixiong, and Christopher Rowland. "Hope: the convergence and divergence of Marxism and liberation theology." *Theology Today* 70, no. 2 (July 2013) 181–95.

Luttio, Mark D. "The Chinese Rites Controversy (1603–1742): A Diachronic and Synchronic Approach." *Worship* 68, no. 4 (July 1994) 290–313.

Macdonald, Charles J-H. "Folk Catholicism and Pre-Spanish Religions in the Philippines." *Philippine Studies* 52, no. 1 (2004) 78–93.

Madsen, William. "Religious Syncretism." In *Social Anthropology: Handbook of Middle American Indians,* vol. 6, edited by Manning Nash, 369–391. Austin, TX: University of Texas Press, 1967.

Malina, Bruce J. "From Isis to Medjugorje: why apparitions?" *Biblical Theology Bulletin* 20, no. 2 (1990) 76–84.

Mattes, Anton. "Devotion to the Heart of Jesus in Modern Times: The Influence of Saint Margaret Mary Alacoque." In *Faith in Christ and the Worship of Christ: New Approaches to Devotion to Christ,* edited by Leo Scheffczyk, translated by Graham Harrison, 101–17. San Francisco: Ignatius, 1986.

McGovern, Arthur F. *Marxism, an American Christian Perspective.* Maryknoll, NY: Orbis, 1980.

McManners, John. *Church and Society in Eighteenth-Century France, vol. 2: The Religion of the People and the Politics of Religion.* Oxford: Oxford University Press, 1999.

McSweeney, Bill. *Roman Catholicism: The Search for Relevance.* New York: St. Martin's, 1980.

Menegon, Eugenio. *Ancestors, Virgins, and Friars: Christianity as a Local Religion in Late Imperial China.* Cambridge, MA: Harvard University Asia Center, 2009. http://www.jstor.org/stable/j.ctt1dnn8nw.

Michalenko, Sophia, CMGT. *The Life of Faustina Kowalska: An Authorized Biography.* Cincinnati: St. Anthony Messenger, 1999.

Minamiki, George. *The Chinese Rites Controversy: From Its Beginning to Modern Times.* Campion Book. Chicago: Loyola University Press, 1985.

Mong, Ambrose Ih-Ren. *Accommodation and Acceptance: An Exploration of Interfaith Relations.* Cambridge: James Clarke, 2015.

———. *Guns and Gospel: Imperialism and Evangelism in China.* Cambridge: James Clarke, 2016.

———. *Purification of Memory: A Study of Modern Orthodox Theologians from a Catholic Perspective.* Cambridge: James Clarke, 2015.

———. *A Tale of Two Theologians: Treatment of Third World Theologies.* Cambridge: James Clark, 2017.

———. "The legacy of Matteo Ricci and his companions." *Missiology* 43, no. 4 (October 2015) 385–97.

Bibliography

———. "Medjugorje Matters." *Ecumenical Trends* 46, no. 9 (October 2017) 1–9, 14.

———. "Our Lady of Guadalupe: model of inculturation." *International Journal for the Study of the Christian Church*, 18:1 9 (2018) 67-83, DOI: 10.1080/1474225X.2018.1493764.

Morgan, David. *The Sacred Heart of Jesus: The Visual Evolution of a Devotion*. Amsterdam: Amsterdam University Press, 2008.

Mungello, David E., Monumenta Serica Institute, and University of San Francisco. Ricci Institute for Chinese-Western Cultural History. *The Chinese Rites Controversy: Its History and Meaning*. Monumenta Serica Monograph Series, no. 33. Nettetal: Steyler Verlag, 1994.

Muse, J. Stephen. "The Bridge Keeper." *The Other Side* 29, no. 2 (1993) 48.

Nash, Manning. *Social Anthropology. Handbook of Middle American Indians*, vol. 6. Austin, TX: University of Texas Press, 1967.

Newman, John Henry. "Lecture 13—On Preaching the Gospel." *Newman Reader*. http://www.newmanreader.org/works/justification/lecture13.html.

———. *Lectures on the Doctrine of Justification*. *Newman Reader*. http://www.newmanreader.org/works/justification/lecture4.html.

———. "Sermon 6—On Justice, as a Principle of Divine Governance." *Newman Reader*. http://www.newmanreader.org/works/oxford/sermon6.html.

———. "Sermon 24—The Religion of the Day." *Newman Reader*. http://www.newmanreader.org/works/parochial/volume1/sermon24.html.

———. *Via Media*. "Preface to the Third Edition." *Newman Reader*. http://www.newmanreader.org/works/viamedia/volume1/preface3.html.

Ortega y Gasset, José. *The Revolt of the Masses*. New York: W. W. Norton & Company, 1932.

Pascal, Blaise. *Pensées*. https://www.gutenberg.org/files/18269/18269-h/18269-h.htm.

Paul VI, Pope. *Evangelii Nuntiandi*. http://w2.vatican.va/content/paul-vi/en/apost_exhortations/documents/hf_p-vi_exh_19751208_evangelii-nuntiandi.html.

———.*Gaudium et spes: Pastoral Constitution on the Church in the Modern World* (December 7, 1965). http://www.vatican.va/archive/hist_councils/ii_vatican_council/documents/vat-ii_const_19651207_gaudium-et-spes_en.html.

———.*Sacrosanctum Concilium: Constitution on the Sacred Liturgy* (December 4, 1963). http://www.vatican.va/archive/hist_councils/ii_vatican_council/documents/vat-ii_const_19631204_sacrosanctum-concilium_en.html.

Phan, Peter C., ed. *Directory on Popular Piety and the Liturgy: Principles and Guidelines: A Commentary*. Collegeville, MN: Liturgical, 2005.

———. "Suffrage for the Dead." In *Directory on Popular Piety and the Liturgy: Principles and Guidelines: A Commentary*, edited by Peter C. Phan. Collegeville, MN: Liturgical Press, 2005.

Pieris, Aloysius. *An Asian Theology of Liberation*. Faith Meets Faith Series. Edinburgh: T. & T. Clark, 1988.

———. "Conversion, controversy and conversation." *Dialogue* (Colombo, Sri Lanka) 9, nos. 1–3 (January 1982) 1–2.

———. *Fire and Water: Basic Issues in Asian Buddhism and Christianity*. Faith Meets Faith. Maryknoll, NY: Orbis, 1996.

———. *Prophetic Humour in Buddhism and Christianity: Doing Inter-Religious Studies in the Reverential Mode*. Colombo: Ecumenical Institute for Study and Dialogue, 2005.

———. *The Genesis of an Asian Theology of Liberation: An Autobiographical Excursus on the Art of Theologizing in Asia*. Gonawala-Kelaniya: Tulana Research Centre, 2013.

Pollard, George. "The Revelation of the Sacred Heart of Jesus Paral-le-Monial, France." *Catholic Culture.* https://www.catholicculture.org/culture/library/view.cfm?recnum=5796.

Poole, Stafford, CM, and Virgilio P. Elizondo. "Guadalupe, Nuestra Señora de." In *The Oxford Encyclopedia of Mesoamerican Cultures.* Oxford: Oxford University Press, 2001. http://www.oxfordreference.com.easyaccess2.lib.cuhk.edu.hk/view/10.1093/acref/9780195108156.001.0001/acref-9780195108156-e-259.

Post, Paulus Gijsbertus Johannes. "Qualities of Ritual: Three Critical Reflections on the Directory on Popular Piety and the Liturgy." *Questions Liturgiques* 88, no. 1 (2007) 24–51.

Ramet, Sabrina P. "The miracle at Medjugorje: a functional perspective." *Religion in Communist Dominated Areas* 25, no. 4 (1986) 170–74.

Ricci, Matteo, and Nicolas Trigault. *China in the Sixteenth Century: The Journals of Matthew Ricci, 1583–1610.* New York: Random House, 1953.

Ricci, Matteo, Douglas Lancashire, Guozhen Hu, and Edward. Malatesta. *The True Meaning of the Lord of Heaven = Tian Zhu Shi Yi.* Chinese-English ed. Series I—Jesuit Primary Sources, in English Translations, no. 6. St. Louis: Institute of Jesuit Sources, 1985.

Ricci, Matteo. *The True Meaning of the Lord of Heaven.* Translated by Douglas Lancashire and Peter Hu Kuo-chen. Taiwan: The Ricci Institute, 1985.

Rios, Matthew. "A continuing theology from the margins: dialogue between Filipino culture and popular religion as a tool for liberation." *Worship* 85, no. 2 (March 2011) 117–27.

Rocca, Francis X. "Pope celebrates diversity of popular piety, unity of church." *Catholic News Service* (May 6, 2013). http://www.catholicnews.com/services/englishnews/2013/pope-celebrates-diversity-of-popular-piety-unity-of-church.cfm.

Rodriquez, Jeanette. *Our Lady of Guadalupe: Faith and Empowerment among Mexican American Women.* Austin, TX: University of Texas Press, 1994.

Ruddy, Christopher. "The Sacred Heart of Jesus." *America* 188, no. 7 (March 3, 2003) 9–11.

Rule, Paul. "Jesuit and Confucian: Chinese religion in the journals of Matteo Ricci, SJ, 1583–1610." *The Journal of Religious History* 5, no. 2 (December 1968) 105–24.

Ryan, Salvador. "Some reflections on theology and popular piety: a fruitful or fraught relationship?" *Heythrop Journal* 53, no. 6 (November 2012) 961–71.

Sala-Boza, Astrid. "Towards Filipino Christian Culture: Mysticism and Folk Catholicism in the Señor Sto. Niño de Cebu." *Philippine Quarterly of Culture and Society* 36, no. 4 (2008) 281–308.

Sapitula, Manuel Victor J. "Marian Piety and Modernity: The Perpetual Help Devotion as Popular Religion in the Philippines." *Philippine Studies: Historical and Ethnographic Viewpoints* 62, no. 3 (2014) 399–424.

Scheffczyk, Leo, ed. *Faith in Christ and the Worship of Christ: New Approaches to Devotion to Christ.* Translated by Graham Harrison. San Francisco: Ignatius, 1986.

Scheffczyk, Leo. "Devotion to Christ as a way of Experiencing him." In *Faith in Christ and the Worship of Christ: New Approaches to Devotion to Christ,* edited by Leo Scheffczyk, translated by Graham Harrison, 207–13. San Francisco: Ignatius, 1986.

Schleiermacher, Friedrich. *On Religion: Speeches to Its Cultured Despisers.* The Cloister Library. New York: Harper, 1958.

Schreiter, Robert J. *Constructing Local Theologies.* Maryknoll, NY: Orbis, 1985.

———. "Culture and inculturation in the church: forty years on dovetailing the gospel with the human kaleidoscope." *New Theology Review* 18, no. 1 (February 2005) 17–26.
Segundo, Juan Luis. *Liberation of Theology*. Maryknoll, NY: Orbis, 1976.
Shelke, Christopher, Mariella Demichele, and Matteo Ricci. *Matteo Ricci in China: Inculturation through Friendship and Faith*. Rome: Gregorian & Biblical, 2010.
Short, Edward. "John Henry Newman in the 'realms of superstition.'" *Newman Studies Journal* 12, no. 2 (September 2015) 46–75.
Sobrino, Jon. *Christ the Liberator: A View from the Victims*. Maryknoll, NY: Orbis, 2001.
———. *Jesus the Liberator: A Historical-Theological Reading of Jesus of Nazareth*. Maryknoll, NY: Orbis, 1993.
Spence, Jonathan D. *The Memory Palace of Matteo Ricci*. New York: Penguin, 1985.
"TAGALOGS Origin Myths, The: Bathala the Creator." *The Aswang Project*. https://www.aswangproject.com/bathala/.
Tracy, David. *Presidential Address to the Catholic Theological Society of America. The Catholic Analogical Imagination (1977)*. https://ejournals.bc.edu/ojs/index.php/ctsa/article/view/2887/2512.
Valeriano, Antonio. "Nican Mopohua: The original XVI Century Guadalupe's Apparition Story" (1560). http://ndclmurray.weebly.com/uploads//3/1/6/2/3162790/nican_mopohua_english.pdf.
Vitz, Rico. "Thomas More and the Christian 'superstition': a puzzle for Hume's psychology of religious belief." *The Modern Schoolman* 88, nos. 3–4 (July 2011) 223–44.
Wiest, Jean-Paul. "Matteo Ricci: pioneer of Chinese-Western dialogue and cultural exchanges." *International Bulletin Of Missionary Research* 36, no. 1 (January 2012) 17–20.
Wiinikka-Lydon, Joseph. "The ambivalence of Medjugorje: the dynamics of violence, peace, and nationalism at a Catholic pilgrimage site during the Bosnian war (1992–1995)." *Journal of Religion & Society* 12, (2010) 1–18.
Wong, Simon K. M. "A Dogmatic and Liturgical Examination of Ancestor Remembrance in the Light of Karl Rahner's Theology of Symbol and its implications on Ecumenism in the Chinese-speaking World." Paper presented at *International Conference on the Asian Ecumenical Movement*, the Chinese University of Hong Kong, April 12–13, 2018.
Young, John D. *East-west Synthesis: Matteo Ricci and Confucianism*. Centre of Asian Studies Occasional Papers and Monographs, No. 44. Hong Kong: Centre of Asian Studies, University of Hong Kong, 1980.
Zialcita, Fernando. "Popular Interpretations of the Passion of Christ." *Philippine Sociological Review* 34, nos. 1–4 (1986) 56–62.
Zimdars-Swartz, Sandra. *Encountering Mary: From La Salette to Medjugorje*. Princeton, NJ: Princeton University Press, 1991.
Zyromski, Page. "Sacramentals: sacred signs of superstitions?" *Catechist* 31 (January 1998) 27–28.

Index

A

Accommodation, xxii, 42, 60–63, 65, 68–70, 78, 83, 96, 108, 142
Adorno, Theodor, 8
Alacoque, Margaret Mary, xxiii, 116–17, 120–26, 130–32, 139
Alienation, 6, 9
All Souls Day, 45, 92, 96
Altamirano, Manual Ignacio, 40
Aquaviva, Rodolfo, 67
Aquinas, Thomas, 74, 78, 117, 119
Aristotle, 78
Auctorem Fidei, 125
Aztec, xxi, 21–28, 30–34, 36–38

B

Barth, Karl, 17
Bathala, 44–45
Bathalang Maykapal, 44
Benedict XVI, Pope, xviii, 36, 94, 101
Bernardino, Juan, 30, 32
Bhattara, 44
Black Nazarene, 46, 49, 54–55, 60
Boff, Leonardo, 2, 9
Bogomil heresy, 103
Bosnia, 97, 103–4, 113–14
Branko, 105
Brundage, Burr C., 25
Buddhism, xx, xxi, 42, 43, 62, 71–74, 76–77, 96
Büntig, Aldo, 11

C

Capitalism, 63
Carroll, Warren, 23, 26, 28
Chaucer, Geoffrey, 144
Ching, Julia, 70
Ching Ming, 95–96
Christendom, 23, 29
Chung, Paul S., 66, 74
Chung Yeung, 96
Clement XI, Pope, 94
Cochin, 67
Colombière, Claude de la, 124
Colonialism, 14, 27, 57, 62
Communism, xxiii, 63, 126
Confucianism, xxii, 62, 66, 70–78
Conscientization, xx, 12, 14
Cortés, Hernán, 21, 23, 25, 28–30
Cosmic, ix, x, 23, 42–44, 55, 75, 83, 85
Cottier, Georges, 136
Cox, Harvey, 2
Croatia, 108, 115
Croiset, 122–23
Cuauhtémoc, 24
Cuitláhuac, 23

D

D'Elia, Pasquale, 68
de Chantal, Jeanne, 117, 120
de Fiore, Joachim, 29
de Gallifet, Joseph, 123
de Ligouri, Alphonsus, 57
de Sales, Francis, 117, 119–20
De servorum Dei beatificatione, 101

Denunciation, 6
Diego, Juan, 19–21, 30–32, 34–37
Dingayan, Luna, 52
Diyos, 45
Dulia, 119
Durkheim, Émile, 108

E

Elizondo, Virgilio P., 26, 37–39
Enlightenment, 77, 132
Erasmus, Desiderius, 80, 86–88
Eucharist, x, xviii, 57, 58, 80, 83, 110, 125, 127, 138, 144
Evangelii nuntiandi, xiii, 3, 64
Extremadura, 21

F

Fatalism, 5, 41, 52
Fatima, xi, xvii, 38, 98–99, 101, 144–45
Ferdinand, King, 24
Fetishism, 5
Flagellation, 54–55, 60
Flores de Mayo, 49
France, 24, 102, 120, 122–24, 126, 128, 139
Franciscans, 29, 30, 34, 98, 103–7

G

Galilea, Segundo, 10
Gante, Pedro de, 33
Gernet, Jacques, 75
Globalization, 63
Gospa, 102, 105, 108
Gramsci, Antonio, 2
Greeley, Andrew, 59–60
Guadalupe, vii, xi, xxi, 19–21, 23, 26, 29, 32–40, 141, 145
Gutiérrez, Gustavo, 1, 11, 13–18
Guzman, Nuño de, 26

H

Haj, 143
Hart, Roger, 75
Haurietis aquas, 126
Hercegovina, 97, 102–4, 106

Hesus Nazareno, 54–55
Hidalgo y Costilla, Miguel de, 39
Hinduism, 42–43
Hong Kong, xiii, xv, xviii, xxii, xxiii, 93, 95, 97, 142–44
Huguenot, 124, 139
Huitzilopochtili, 22

I

Icons, 138
Ideology, xi, 7, 10, 13, 70, 113
Idolatry, xii, xx, xxii, 29, 64, 89–90, 92
Imitation of Christ, 56, 128
Imperialism, 14, 63
Inculturation, vii, x, xix, xxii, 21, 33, 34, 35, 40, 60–62, 65, 78, 83, 91, 142
Isabella, Queen, 24

J

Jansen of Ype, Cornelius, 124
Jansenists, 123–24
John Paul II, Pope, xii, 32, 35–36, 44, 62, 78, 98, 130, 134–40
Joyeux, Henry, 113

K

K'ang-his, 74
Katipunan, 53
Kingdom of God, 16–17, 63
Kipling, Rudyard, 62
Kowalska, Faustina, 116, 128
Kumbh Mela, 143

L

La Salette, 99
la Vega, Laso de, 39
Las Casas, Bartholomé, 28
Latria, 119
Laurentin, René, 112–13
Liberative evangelization, 1, 12
Liturgy, xvii, xviii, xix, xxii, 3, 5, 9, 10, 33, 56, 58, 65, 80–83, 85, 91, 95, 127, 136, 138, 140
Lord of Heaven, 35, 62, 71–74, 76–78
Lourdes, xi, xvii, 38, 98, 99, 101, 143–44

Index

M

Magellan, Ferdinand, 46, 50, 51
Mahāyāna, 71, 76
Marx, Karl, 6
Marxism, xx, 10, 62, 104
Mass Religion, 7
Mediator Dei, 82
Medjugorje, vii, xi, xiii, xxii, xxiii, 38, 97–99, 101–3, 105–15, 142
Mestiza, 35
Metacosmic, ix, x, xi, 42–43
Mexico, xiii, xxi, 3, 20–25, 27–30, 32–40, 141, 145
Ming Dynasty, 66, 71, 76
Modernism, 62
Montesinos, Antonio de, 28
Montezuma, 23, 28
Montmartre, Basilica, 122

N

Nahuatl-, 22
Newman, John Henry, vi, 80–81, 88–90, 92
Nican Mopohua, 37, 39
Niebuhr, Richard R., 143
Novena Church, 145–46

O

Oppression, 1, 3–5, 9, 11, 15, 17–18, 41, 52–53
Oršolić, Marko, 114
Ortega y Gasset, José, 8, 11

P

Paganism, 50
Panginoon, 45
Paray-le-Monial, 120, 123
Paschal mystery, 5, 42, 85, 91, 145
Pasyon, 47, 54
Paul VI, John, xiii, 17, 64
Penafrancia, Our Lady of, 47, 49
Perić, Ratko, 102, 106–7
Perpetual Help, Our Lady of, xxii, 41, 56
Phan, Peter, xvi, 81

Philippines, The, xiii, xxi, 2, 40–46, 48, 50–52, 54, 56–57, 59–60, 141, 144
Pieris, Aloysius, ix, 42–44
Pilgrimages, ix, xi, xv, xvii, xxiii, 102, 106–7, 142–44
Pius XI, Pope, 126
Pius XII, Pope, 82, 94, 101, 126
Political reductionism, 15
Poole, Stafford, 39
Populorum Progressio, 17
Portuguese, 66–70
Protestantism, xxiii, 29, 51, 124, 139
Puebla, 3–5, 9–10, 14

Q

Quetzalcóatl, 22, 25
Quiapo, 46–47, 54

R

Rahner, Karl, 62
Redemptoris Missio, 44
Redemptorists, 58
Reformation, 29, 65, 100, 124
Ricci, Matteo, x, xxii, 60, 62, 65–78, 142
Rites Controversy, xxii, 68, 78, 81, 90–94
Ritualism, 5
Rituals, ix, x, xi, xvii, 45, 70, 87, 92, 96, 144
Rodriguez, Jeanette, 26
Ruggieri, Michele, 70, 72

S

Sacramentals, 85–86
Sacred Heart, vii, xi, xvii, xxiii, 115–17, 119–27, 132, 134–35, 138–40, 142
Sacrosanctum Concilium, 82
Santo Niño, xxii, 41, 50–55, 60, 141
Scheffczyk, Leo, 127
Second Vatican Council, 16, 135, 140
Secularism, 63, 126
Segundo, Juan Luis, 7–8
Sensus Fidelium, 38, 83
Sinulog, 46, 49
Slovenia, 113
Solidarity, xviii, 4, 7, 9, 13–15, 18, 60, 97–98, 127

Sopocko, Michael, 133, 139
Soteriology, 42
Spaniards, 21, 23–27, 30, 33–35, 40, 42, 52, 69
Superstitions, 5, 77, 87–88, 90
Syncretism, 2, 9, 33–34, 36, 41, 51, 57, 61, 65, 76, 81

T

Tagal, 45
Taoism, 42, 62, 72, 76, 96
Tenochtitlán, 22, 35
Tepeyac, 20–21, 30–32, 35–37, 40
Teresa, of Lisieux, 129
Texcoco, 22, 30, 33
Tilma, 21, 32, 35, 37
Tlacopan, 22
Tlaloc, 22
Tonatiuh, 22
Tracy, David, 59
Tres de Abril, 53

Trinity, 77, 127, 138, 140
Tzcóatl, 22

U

Utopia, 12–14

V

Valignano, Alessandro, 68–69, 72
Via Media, 88
Visitation, Order, 117, 120
Vladec, Janco, 104

W

Wong, Simon, 93

Z

Žanić, Pavao, 106–7
Zimdars-Swartz, Sandra, 100
Zumárraga, Juan de, 20, 30–32

www.ingramcontent.com/pod-product-compliance
Lightning Source LLC
Chambersburg PA
CBHW021914180426
43198CB00035B/585